LACK OR SUCCESS

Also by Brian Rassi

MeFormula: Personalized Solutions Made Easy®

LACK OR SUCCESS

A Step-by-Step Guide for Aligning Your Purpose,
Raising Your Consciousness, and Transforming
Your Experiences to Turn Failure into Success!

BRIAN RASSI

Printed in the United States of America

Published by Author Academy Elite
PO Box 43, Powell, OH 43035
www.AuthorAcademyElite.com

Library of Congress Cataloging: 2021907668
ISBN: 978-1-64746-774-6 (paperback)
ISBN: 978-1-64746-775-3 (hardback)
ISBN: 978-1-64746-776-0 (eBook)
Available in paperback, hardback, e-book, and audiobook

TENFOUR
MEDIA GROUP

Book Design Cover and interior images design by
Carey Matlin, Ten Four Media Group LLC.

To my best friend, life partner, spiritual teacher and love, Imelda Arcilla. You came into my life years ago and I am so grateful for that.

May this book be a small token of my deepest affection for you, your wisdom, and the many lasting memories of your experiences while you were here on earth.

CONTENTS

PART 3
WHEN FAILURE SHOWS UP YOU NEED TO UNLACK

PART 4
HOW TO NAVIGATE AND TURN FAILURE INTO SUCCESS

PART 5
CHOOSE MASTERY AND HOW BEST TO IMPLEMENT

APPENDICES

FOREWORD

You have been lied to. You're not broken, you don't need fixing, you just need an education.

An education to wake up the power that is inside of you. This powerful energetic force is able to create miracles, yet in most of us, it lays dormant.

We stay asleep to our power, believing we don't have it in us to be a success. We have been conditioned to believe we are broken and separate from this source of power inside of us, it is not true.

I started out in a working-class family from a small country on the bottom of the world, now I have two companies that make over $10 million dollars each, I am known by millions around the world and live a life I once dreamed of, and so can you!

How? By reading books like the one you have in your hand, working with mentors and doing whatever it takes. To seek out knowledge on how to uncover and live from this powerful place. Which is a noble quest and one that should be put at the highest of all priorities.

Even better than knowledge is to find mentors who can shorten the learning curve and help you on the path. This is what Brian is, he walks the talk and can show you exactly how to uncover your true gifts and create a RICH Life.

No matter where you start from, you have the ability to create magic and turn all your dreams into reality, however, you must follow through!!!

Read this book, apply the learnings, and take aligned action.

With Love,

Christopher M. Duncan [1]
Founder of *The Magnetic Mind Method*
CEO of *The Conscious Education Company*
Author of *You're Not Broken*

PREFACE AND INTRODUCTION

"MAGIC doesn't happen on the well-traveled path!"
—Imelda Arcilla [2]

"Brian, you know magic doesn't happen on the well-traveled path. You will find your path to success, and it will come when you remember you are already a Master!"

When Imelda told me this, it instantly connected on multiple levels. My eyes began to tear, and I could feel myself getting very emotional for some reason. It was like she was speaking to a person I could only desire to become one day.

I was broke–financially, emotionally, mentally, and physically. I experienced another business failure a month earlier, and I was so busy trying to do anything I could to make a little bit of money to keep from getting evicted from our home at the time.

For years, I had been so successful in everything I had ever set my mind to, but now, something was wrong. Something was very wrong. How could I go from a six-figure a year status, own my home, own a rental property, and have $80,000+ saved to being completely broke?

My failures didn't end there. They continued until the answers to all my questions started to reveal themselves to me. Time and time again, I would get something going only to have it ripped away from me in a blink of an eye by the most unexpected circumstances, or so I thought.

Have you ever experienced a pain so intense it completely shattered your world? I remember that moment for me, and it came in June 2017 when I lost my beloved muse, Imelda Arcilla. Imelda, in my eyes, was a complete force for good who could defy the laws of nature. Suddenly, she was gone, leaving a gaping void within my most sacred emotions and beliefs.

She was my best friend, my lover, my spiritual teacher, my secret weapon, my business partner, and truly one of the wisest people I have ever met on this planet. Anyone who met her over the years would tell you the same thing about her. She was really that special of a person.

About three weeks after Imelda had passed, I realized I was completely lost, and my whole self-identity was shattered. The deep pain and sorrow was suffocating me into depths of emotions. I even had brief thoughts of suicide.

I didn't realize I possessed the ability to think this way. But then, a flash of inspiration popped into my mind, and I thought of Imelda's RICH Playbook course.[3] That one thought changed everything.

RICH is an acronym for Reclaim your Integrity to Create Happiness. This course is simple and powerful. It teaches how you can't live a successful life until you are able to feel happy in all areas of your life. I retook the course, and something magical started to happen as I went through it again. I was connecting to information in a way like never before. I was open, I was vulnerable, and I was seeking relief from the current circumstances.

Imelda had a saying: "Turn your focus from being scared to a sacred being that you truly are!" That was exactly what I was feeling over the following days. Thoughts, events, experiences, insights, signs, people, circumstances, and situations kept popping up and pushing me to move forward toward living my happiness. Over the next couple of weeks, months, and now closing on years, I have been following these synchronistic events. As I think back, I feel like I actually won the lottery when I remembered Imelda's program!

During this time, the answers to many questions that have alluded me for over a decade came into focus through tracing back over the painful experiences. Each unraveled a piece or a clue to how it would be possible to find my path to success. Through this quest to the truth, there have been too many unexplained events which led me to share my insights with you as well. You don't have to experience the pain of failure in your life any longer.

Before we go into the many twists and turns that were necessary to shape my perspective over the years, I need to fill you in with my insider viewpoint of Imelda. I reference Imelda throughout the book for multiple reasons, and I feel it's imperative for you to know why and to get to know her a little bit better.

I first met her in February 2004 at the Fairfield Resorts in Pompano Beach, FL.[4-5] I was training to become a sales executive to offer timeshare packages. As part of my training, we would learn the psychology of the customer and go out on a real-life tour with an experienced sales executive to observe all the many steps of the presentation to get better acquainted with the process.

I got out late from training and was the last one to be placed with someone to ride with. The tours were already underway for the morning, and the manager walked me over to a table where the potential customer got up to get a cup of coffee. She wanted me to join in on this tour and she introduced me to Imelda.

Imelda was five feet one inch tall, barely 100 pounds, with an exotic Filipino (from one of the islands) look that would truly captivate you. Before the potential customer came back to the table, Imelda sized me up and looked directly in my eyes and said with a straight face, "Don't say a fu*king word on my tour."

All I did after she said that was nod my head and sit down at the table. I was truly taken aback by her beauty and gravitas to tell it exactly like it is. Some people would see her outer beauty and try to classify her as just another pretty girl. Anyone that was able to look past her striking outer features would find an even more attractive inner essence and wisdom.

She was a combination of Indiana Jones, Lara Croft, Oprah, Richard Branson, and Buddha.[6-10] What amazed me even more about her was her ability to face incredible pain and immense pressure to somehow find a way to navigate us through any difficult situation with utter calmness. Her presence alone was able to shift the outcome of most situations in many areas of our lives.

Over our initial year (2004) of getting to know each other, Imelda began to open up to me about her intuitive abilities.

At first, I was taken aback by her story and quickly realized without a shadow of a doubt Imelda was able to tap into information not readily available to the common man or woman.

In the early 2000s, she had an out of body mystical experience that truly changed the landscape of her life forever. This experience allowed her to come to understand that the universe is inside each and every one of us. She learned that everything we're searching for is within, waiting to be activated through desires and experiences.

Ever since this event, Imelda, through the course of her daily activities, would be able to unpack this information, which is love, wisdom, and intelligence, along with some divine magic. This divine magic was what Imelda and I were most interested in getting to know more about over our 14+ physical years together.

As the years went by, Imelda became, to me and many others, a wise sage. She was the go-to person for any situation to get the truth and, more importantly, the right next step to take to move forward with your life no matter what was being expressed in the physical form.

She has a powerful and loving energy about her. Her holistic approach and non-conventional way of accessing information went much, much deeper in an interconnected level, way beyond the surface. This allows her the ability to assess others through her wisdom to discover their greatest potential and destiny.

I'm a natural seeker of truth and have always been curious to anything that catches my eye. Imelda caught my third eye–the eye that stares directly into your soul. I believe you need to open this third eye to find yourself and realize success.

Throughout the book, you will begin to witness some of the many instances where Imelda was able to showcase her innate wisdom to me, and now, to you as well. For anyone out there who would ask "if she was so gifted, why wasn't she already a well-known star or guru?"

I can tell you it wasn't because we never tried. Much of my success in business came from her innate insight, clarity, and inner confidence through real-life experiences. Ask anyone who met her over the years, and they will all tell you Imelda was, and still is, a major force in their lives.

It was one of my supposedly many failures over the years of not being able to provide her the physical experience of playing on a much bigger stage. Through the course of this journey, after the fact with much hindsight, her success is very much validated through the wisdom she left behind as you will witness and experience over the course of the book.

"It's not what you do. It's who you are."
—Mike Dooley [11]

As for me, it has been a very long and tedious road to be able to fully understand the gravity of my experience up to this point. I never realized the magnificent journey I was truly on until many things I took for granted was taken away from me. In my own journey to rediscover my true self and purpose I realized that I was also influencing those around me to do the same.

My journey to find success again in my life was the impetus to so much being revealed to me that I could not sit silent any longer. This information had to be shared, otherwise, it would have been misused knowledge and wisdom to create my own life instead of fueling those around me to create their's as well.

I was born into a wonderful and loving family who raised me with sound Midwest values while being influenced by our family's cultural, ancestral beliefs, and viewpoints as you will find out throughout the book. My mom was 100% Lebanese, and my dad was mostly German with a little Swiss and French. Ironically, with this mixture of nationalities and skin color, combined with our last name being Rassi, people assumed I was Italian. (I recently took a DNA test to finally figure it out. Not only am I Lebanese, German, and French, but also Italian and British. Who knew.)

To many on the outside looking in, we were in the top percentages of society financially with a big home on a private lake and all the comforts you would expect with that status. Underneath it all we were trapped in a wicked financial failure cycle that so many must go through in order to find that everlasting success they naturally yearn for. Little did I realize that I was going to follow in a very similar cycle later on in life.

I was around six when we moved from that really large home into a very small rental. My dad was involved in a business failure where he personally signed for a note and the bank called it. The loan amount was too large of an amount to overcome.

That unfortunate circumstance forced my parents to downsize and face financial strains that many people know all too well. We moved from place to place as my dad began to get promoted within his company. Oddly enough, this was beneficial to me. It became the building blocks of my insatiable drive for stability and success.

Over time, I developed an outgoing personality combined with an outstanding work ethic, a passion for sports and a knack of meeting new people. This allowed me to thrive in grade school and high school. I had a natural ability to lead, relate, and communicate well with other people. My drive to work hard, play hard, and strive for more became an internal quest to accomplish something of great significance. I came here to enjoy the full experience of life and boy that was what I set my mind to do.

Like so many of us at that age, we simply don't know where to correctly focus our emotions, thoughts, and energy. I did my best to do what felt natural to me. In high school, I gravitated towards sports and quickly became a prominent (Captain on multiple teams, VP of my Class for three years, and Homecoming King) person in anything I focused my energy on.

Ultimately in college, I channeled my energy into leadership roles with the fraternity and spent most of my time working my way up to one of the head bartenders of the biggest bar in the Big Ten, once again finding a way to obtain success in both school and financially. I had plenty of money from tips to do what I wanted whenever I wanted in college.

Overall, both high school and college were amazing experiences for me. This led right into my first career position with KONE.[12] After three to four years of hard work, I was promoted to sales manager of our San Diego[13] office. On the outside, this was a great career success, but on the inside, something was missing. I knew this wasn't the right path for me.

I quit and moved across the country in search of my right path. This move raised many fears within me, my friends, and my family. I remember a distinct conversation with my Dad about this move and he warned me of a possible rough road ahead. I was in search of something more to experience and I was determined to get it.

Within one month I met Imelda, and within two to three years I quickly rose up the ranks of Wells Fargo Home Mortgage South Florida Division.[14] That's when I began to unconsciously feel the ever-growing challenges of the residential loan market beginning to surface.

Out of fear of failure and the need to expand my loan product offers, an opportunity to start up a unique alternative finance company popped up unexpectedly. I left Wells Fargo to pursue my entrepreneurial desires and hopefully find a more diverse way to make money.

Little did I know at the time, it was less than a year away from the 2008 financial crisis that rocked the entire country.[15] When that happened, I began to pivot and chase the money in many of the wrong areas and with many of the wrong people.

This led me on a ten-year cycle of many failures, business ventures, millions of dollars raised, breakthroughs, set-backs, ah-ha moments, partnerships, and many well-deserved experiences that have helped me persevere into a seasoned entrepreneur and professional in my field today.

No one wants to go through adversity, pain, failure, mistakes, and the many setbacks Imelda and I experienced over the past many years together. I can assure you, if it all went well, I wouldn't be here talking about this topic of failure.

Deep down inside I knew this topic needed to be addressed from this very unique angle. The benefit that has come from it has been truly overwhelming for me personally because I know it will help you along your unique journey as well. That is a very gratifying feeling to experience.

Let's set some expectations about what this book is and what it isn't. I'm not a psychologist, scientist, guru, priest, millionaire (yet), and/or a Shaolin monk. This is not going to be a display of my intelligence because that was never my goal. I wanted to find a way to achieve success again like I did for the past 30+ years before the failures began to surface. Maybe you can relate in some way.

I have read many books, paid for coaches, spiritual readings, sought out specialists, went to seminars, watched videos, and spent thousands of dollars and many more hours trying to get out of this self-spiral of never-ending failures. But never during the entire process of ten plus years of constant searching did anyone piece together the entire cycle of failure in a simple to understand format, and most importantly, how to find a path to success from it.

I decided to map it out for myself. In that process of mapping it out and implementing practical daily exercises, I began to see results. As the results began to manifest in my life, I would continue to tweak my daily regimen with the new relevant information I was gathering to see if I could continue to achieve more of my dreams.

As time continued to pass and goals continued to be achieved, I began to share my insights with close friends, selected family members, and business associates. As they began to read the book and share their insights, the overall response was that this information would help others succeed. So, here we are.

I know what world we live in these days—it's a result-driven society. You want to know what the benefits will be after reading this book. The results I speak about will be different for you because we all have different aspirations and dreams we want to achieve in life. The list below is what I was able to achieve as of the latest version of the book.

- Able to feel my emotions and change them to feel better in the moment.
- Able to consciously think and control my thoughts more often.
- I know who I am and am able to feel happiness for longer periods of time.
- Understand the right next step to take to achieve my desire.
- Lost over 40+ pounds of weight and kept it off since.
- Started a successful business and love what I do every day.
- Changed my thoughts which allowed me to change my life.
- Reconnected with my family, friends, and loved ones.
- Attract all the right people and answers on demand.
- And many more you will read about within the rest of the book.

I remember how hard Imelda worked each day reading, connecting, writing, contemplating, training, teaching, and pushing the boundaries of understanding what is really going on in this world. I considered her lifestyle closer to what a modern-day monk would be like if they traveled from the Tibetan Mountain into any major city.

She literally would do readings for me every day and try to do her best to get me interested in the daily work required to reconnect to my intuition. It's hard to be motivated when you have a spiritual crutch living with you. It was much more convenient to ask for a reading then it was to do it myself.

I promised myself I would live a rich and successful life. I would do whatever was necessary to develop my skills to the point where I could obtain that connection to knowledge again and have complete faith in my ability to do so. Every day, I continue to push the boundaries to uncover another layer of understanding and feel I will be doing this till the day I leave earth as well.

During my quest to figure it out, I heavily relied on the knowledge and expertise of many well-known individuals you have definitely heard of. What I would do is research and then implement something into my daily life.

"To know and not to do is really not to know."
—Stephen Covey [16]

Something magical began to happen ever so slightly. As the days, weeks, and months kept coming and going, my daily habits changed as well. As this change was happening, I decided to document the flow of life all around me until a pattern began to form.

I would write down a goal or a desire I would want to accomplish and then wait to see how it would come to fruition. Sure enough, my thoughts began to translate into the people, circumstances, situations, and media showing up in my daily life. I kept expanding until many of the pieces of the cycle of failure and success were documented.

A good tip for getting the most out of this book is to have a physical notebook or journal available to write out items you want to remember. The actual physical action of writing helps you engage certain areas of your brain.

Once you understand the cycle of failure and all its reasons for showing up in your life, a wonderful thing will occur. You will no longer be afraid of it and, in fact, you will begin to reframe it so you can tap into the MAGIC to experience more daily successes in your life.

This is my definition of RICH living.

RICH Living - Goal

- The ability to experience more success and happiness in your life.

Now that I have documented enough tangible results in my life, it's time to pass along this information to those specific individuals who choose to experience the same and hopefully much better.

This book will cover the root causes to all failure and how to solve them when you encounter them in the future to experience a successful outcome. Everything is backed by science, research, and real-life experience showing that there is more to life than meets the eye when you become devoted to the magical transformational process of creation.

I recently made a large commission from helping a client get a business loan. I was feeling really good about the business and decided to ramp up the marketing to attract more scheduled phone calls. I interviewed many companies and decided to go with a company who had a full-service approach to getting me scheduled calls.

They happened to be the most expensive service I came across, but I wanted to have the peace of mind that I would get the calls I needed. I gave them all the copy and articles, and they wrote excellent copy based on my words and began to market to thousands of business owners and entrepreneurs.

After a month, I got concerned because I wasn't getting phone calls, so we tweaked the messaging and still no phone calls. I'm an optimist and voiced positivity, but after thousands of dollars spent and thousands of people marketed to, I got a whopping three phone calls!

This was not good, especially since I had no revenue, and my resources were dwindling. I put the campaign on hold and began to see a silver lining in my epic marketing failure. That business model and messaging was taking me down a path that wasn't going to help me attract the right people for me to talk to.

Within one to two months of applying my daily practices outlined in this book to this situation, I was able to revamp my company and attract the right people to help me fulfill my vision. If I didn't have that failure that early on it would have taken me so much longer to find the right business path for success.

Every day we experience many failures on multiple levels. Some failures are directly related to you specifically and some are indirectly related. Regardless, they are happening all around us. These failures shape us and mold us through the lessons derived from experiencing them.

Often, they redirect us on a path less traveled that is very unique to you. How you see the world would be totally different than how I see the world, even if we experienced the same failure directly. The experience of failure becomes the impetus for a change to take place.

This book was written with a specific intention to serve as a guide to better explain how you can choose and master success in your life in achieving your dreams. I wanted to pull back the curtain on the topic of failure which seems to be the pink elephant in the room in most households, schools, and businesses these days.

Many people are literally and most definitely afraid of even thinking about the failures that have occurred in their lives. The stigma that even thinking or speaking about failures will have an effect on future successes is totally false. Actually, it is paralyzing for most people until they understand the full picture and know what it all entails.

Only then can they see the game of nature unfolding right in front of them on full display. The interactions with every person, article, social media post, business associate, significant other, and anything else will become a true reflection of your desired success.

This is a *proven* path for anyone who is interested in achieving their full potential by taking responsibility for their personal and professional growth. Regardless of their past, current or future circumstances, they can have a simple to understand road map to achieve success in whatever area they want that will work, no matter what!

To master your craft, you must first understand what failure actually is, why it shows up in our lives, and most importantly, how to use it to find your path to success.

I can hear some of you talking to yourself right now saying, "I don't want to learn about failure. I want to only experience success. I don't want to even think about failure ever again. I only want to think about success, that's it!" Only when we remove lack can we unlock more success in our life. That will become your reality only after you have mastered the basics that we will cover in this book.

This book will give you the information you can immediately use in your life and business. It is your job to continue to work at it. Let me tell you a story from Kevin Trudeau. It is about a Shaolin Monk who was a master in the art of Kung Fu. The monk said, "I'm not afraid of the 10,000 strikes you have practiced once, I'm afraid of the one punch you can throw and have practiced 10,000 times." [17-18]

This, at its very core, is my entire premise of how you can experience success in your life on a daily basis. ***Mastery of success is truly mastery of failure as well.***[19] You can't have one without the other. I know this is a crazy idea for some. For those who decide to seek a proven path going forward, today is your day.

I'm a firm believer that everything happens for a particular reason. If you're here reading at this moment, take that as a major sign from your higher self that something I'm about to write is supposed to be presented to you.

I promise you even the most well-read and well-educated individual who writes, trains, and coaches people in this field of failure, transformation, and success in some way will get something out of this book.

It could be as simple as an answer to a question you have been seeking to receive. It could be that you are meant to begin down a new path toward your success. Or it could be that we were meant to simply exchange energies for some reason that will become known to the both of us in the future at an appropriate time.

MAGIC doesn't happen on the well-traveled path. Imelda's MAGIC acronym and definition was "Multi-dimensional Alignment with God's Infinite Creation." [20] Only recently have I been able to fully understand what she meant by this, and by the end of the book, you will as well.

The way Imelda interacted with the world around her was different than the way I interacted with mine. She had an inner knowing, a way of processing the underlying truth behind the outer world perception of a situation. It seemed magical how she did things.

I always wondered if I would be able to see the world from a similar point of view. She always told me that I would one day, and that anyone could if they worked at it. Now you can too because by mastering the basics this wonderful world will open up to you in a magical way that I promise you is worth it.

You were meant to get this information and to experience more of what you desire because of it. You will find your path to success, and it will come when you remember you are already a master.

PART 1

Clarity on the Underlying Root Cause of Failure

CHAPTER 1

FEAR OF FAILURE OR FEAR OF SUCCESS? HOW ABOUT NEITHER!

"Affirmations don't make something happen; they make something welcome."
—Michael Beckwith [21]

I was walking one day, and I was going through my daily affirmations during the walk when a flash of intuition struck about the framework of failure. It truly laid out the way it works in our life. Many people allow fear in their life to dictate how far they will go.

Understanding the power of fear and how it controls our lives is key. Everyone understands fear, and in our culture, most people gravitate toward what they feel they know to be true. They feel that fear is the driving force behind their failure or success. What if they are wrong in this assumption?

What if failure is the root to all change in our lives? Some of us can talk about fear and be able to process that information without it affecting our emotional state, but for many, that is not possible. If we run away from the opportunity to talk about fear, what do you think happens when we bring up the subject of failure?

That's right, this unknown and undiscussed topic of failure is shunned by most people. This is done to the devilish demise of their subconscious and unconscious mind which dictates their every move. When left unnoticed, it has the ability to spread and multiply so quickly into many areas of our lives. Until . . . we are able to bring it to light and set it free.

Let's take the first step to choosing success by understanding the definition of failure.

failure (fālyər/noun)

1. lack of success.
   a. Synonyms: lack of success, nonfulfillment, defeat, collapse, foundering, etc.
2. the omission of expected or required action.

The key word in the definition of failure is "lack." This "lack" will manifest and show up in our everyday lives. Lack of direction, money, love, relationships, companionship, meaning, partnership, awareness, impact, expectation, results, success, joy, time, motivation, productivity, sales, attention, focus, employee turnover, legacy, and the list goes on.

Is this why both sayings, fear of failure and fear of success, are wrong? They aren't what drive us to do what we do. It is the *lack* in our lives that drives us to do what we do.

I remember the moment distinctly when I allowed fear to get the best of me. I was a home mortgage consultant in South Florida. I was doing well on the outside, but something started to shift on the inside. I recently bought an investment property and had trouble getting it rented. The rental property wasn't in the local area. It was a thousand miles away from where I currently lived, which wasn't an ideal situation. For months it sat vacant, and I couldn't get in rented.

The paying of two mortgages was starting to weigh on me without the extra income of my rental property. I took on a weak renter and that helped a little bit until they couldn't afford to pay anymore. This was the beginning of the fear filling up inside. In my business, I had some loans going, but the market was shifting.

I could feel the underwriting department becoming more stringent. A recent hurricane came through and totally stopped loans from closing for 30 days, and I knew right then and there it was going to get rough in the residential home market.

I was paying for a secretary with my boss. I was fixated on cutting back her pay to save money. My mind jumped to thinking I need to focus on getting more loans. Then it jumped to thinking that even if I get more loans, if they don't close, I still don't get paid. Then the phone rang, and it was a potential business deal to get into alternative lending. I was all ears!

As I think back on this moment in time, it was clear that I was letting the feeling of fear dictate what my next decision was going to be. I didn't recognize how the feeling of fear was only a symptom to a much deeper insidious inner vibration of lack.

That decision to jump into a new business was the impetus to many failures in my life for over a decade. I was mentally, emotionally, physically, spiritually, and financially not ready to make the jump. Regardless of my readiness, I jumped anyway.

Let's dig deep into this subject of lack because once it is understood, it sets the foundation to recognizing what is driving you to do what you do each day. Like in my story above, it was lack of money that was driving my decision, not fear as you're about to see below.

Upon further study, it is the lack of financial security that can impede one's IQ as well. In 2013, *The Journal of Science* published a study which indicated that, on average, a person preoccupied with money problems exhibited a drop in cognitive function similar to a 13-point dip in IQ, or the loss of an entire night's sleep.[22-23]

These studies were based on the premise of how one's cognitive decisions are influenced due to lack of money. Would it be any different if we were lacking love? Could that be the reason why someone would cheat on their significant other? What about lack of support? Could that be the reason why a business partner could do something unthinkable to sabotage the success of the company? What about lack of confidence? Could that be the reason why someone hides away in their home not wanting to go out into the world with others?

The study concludes people who are experiencing lack of money lose the ability to think clearly. The study also showed once the person received money back into their life, they were able to raise their cognitive function back up to normal and make much better decisions.[24] This is no different when you receive support and love. It helps you feel good, which allows you to think better as well.

The second portion of the definition of failure is the "omission of the expected." As you can see, the omission of the expected doesn't always have to be about you and your actions directly.

It can happen indirectly from a third party or from the other person as well.

For example, think about your reaction if you were working hard for a promotion in your career but someone else got the position ahead of you. Your expectations would dictate if that event was a failure. If you really felt you were the right candidate, being overlooked might either irritate you or light a fire within you to become better qualified to get the next promotion.

Finally, you get promoted after you worked so hard for a couple of years. On the outside it is considered a success, but on the inside, you lacked enjoyment on the journey to get the promotion. By the definition above, you failed in this endeavor because your driving force behind the journey in the first place was the feeling of satisfaction not recognition.

How long will it be before the lack calls you to do something to release the pressure as it builds up and overwhelms you? Will it drive you to the point of making a decision such as quitting the job all together or justifying to yourself that another company might be better suited for your skill set?

Doesn't this shed a new light on why you truly do the things you do? Doesn't this sound like what commonly happens in a mid-life crisis? Or does this give you a better insight on the millennial generation in the workplace?

This is being supported more and more by millennial generation job statistics.[25-27] The main reasons why millennials are changing careers and employers so often is lack of culture and/or lack of fit. The work environment is lacking balance, lacking stimulation, lacking growth opportunities, and lacking the ability to earn more for the desired workload.

This generation of workers and employers are suffering from many failures at an unprecedented rate on a daily basis. Let's look at the small business and entrepreneurial world.

Over 50% of the working population (120 million individuals) works in a small business. Small businesses have generated over 65% of the net new jobs since 1995. Approximately 543,000 new businesses get started each month (but more employer businesses shut down than start up each month); seven out of ten new employer firms survive at least two years, half at least five years, a third at least ten years, while a quarter stay in business 15 years or more.[28-29]

No matter if it is a lack of money, lack of customers, lack of good management decisions, or a lack of fulfillment, the underlying pain is *lack*. When we feel this lack, it is causing us to recognize it as a form of failure. That failure expresses itself in many different ways from fear, to quitting work, to not sleeping, to emotional distress, filling up your mental bandwidth, not generating enough cash flow, and the list goes on.

This pain in the form of lack is not the real problem in my eyes. It is the byproduct of something even bigger going on. There are plenty of statistics and many more personal experiences to justify that failure is happening all around us. Many people have spent an exorbitant amount of time trying to help others with their failures over the years. Could it be many of them have been missing the mark on the best way to do it?

How do you change something if you are not really aware of the many aspects going on behind the scenes? Obviously, whatever is currently being expressed out in the world for others to learn and grow from doesn't seem to be stopping the many failures happening in our lives. In fact, it could be safe to say we are failing with our expectations on this subject which is the real reason you gravitated toward this book in the first place.

To remove lack (aka *unlack*), you must first understand fundamentally what, why, and how failure functions in our daily lives.

Unlack (/un-lack/adjective)

1. To remove lack

Second, you must learn and practice the process of how to align, raise, and transform failure into a success.

In basic terms we must transform the lack into what you desire to experience. To do this, we first must understand the definition of lack.

Lack (/lak/noun)

1. the state of being without or not having enough of something.

As you can see, when we're without or not having enough of something, it causes us to take notice of it energetically even if you don't know about it physically. Whatever is in lack will capture the attention of the individual causing a perpetual rendezvous to take place until the lack is filled.

I remember crying on my drive home from work one night thinking about my life, Imelda, and if this career path was for me. As I cried and talked out loud to her (Imelda had passed away), I could feel this comfort come over me. I remember a conversation we once had, regarding a previous job of mine that required me to go door-to-door.

At that time, we were living with her parents. We had little money, and I really disliked going door-to-door. I remember I broke down crying in the car while I was out in the field. I struggled to get appointments and sales. I was new to this business and the fear of failure was getting the best of me.

I knew I needed to make money to get us out of our current situation. I was overcome by the circumstances as well. Everything in my mind and body wished I would simply throw in the towel. But how could I go home to Imelda and look her in the eye, heck, look myself in the eye, if I quit?

I called her from the field, and I was sitting in a parking lot contemplating if I could keep doing this or not. As I got on the phone, I broke down crying because I was afraid, scared, stressed, tired, and completely overwhelmed by the situation. I was stuck and allowed my ego and logical mindset to get the best of me.

Imelda was gifted. She was a professional intuitive and specialized in mindset situations like mine. I told her all of the valid points as to why I was scared and why I should quit. She listened and then said something that changed the course of my career, and our lives, instantly.

"Turn your focus from being scared to a sacred being that you truly are!" Holy smokes! That line shook me to my core! Then she said, "Brian, you need to get out of the car and finish what you started. I promise you, if you do that, something amazing is going to happen because of it. You are more than just a door-to-door salesman, and if you do this with everything you have, there will come a time in the near future when you will realize that!"

Long story short, I went to the next shopping plaza where I set my first two appointments for my new career that day. Fast forward a couple of days later, I made my first two sales to those people totaling $2,000.00 in commissions. That money allowed us the ability to move to a new city where I became a manager very quickly. Our lives changed that day because I listened to Imelda's advice.

As I cried while driving home and talking to her, I remembered that conversation she'd had with me. The comfort that came over me was the realization that this situation was exactly the same situation I'd had years earlier. All I needed to do was realize I'm in the right place, at the right time, with the right people around me.

All I needed to do was wake up the next day and get out of the car and finish what I started. Imelda promised me if I do that, something amazing is going to happen because of it!

As you can see, this memory of mine with Imelda on two separate occasions clearly shows the lack in my life both times. My decisions between these events were still being driven by lack as well.

In my case, it was showing up in lack of confidence and lack of trust which was expressing itself in the form of fear. The fear was causing me to react emotionally, physically, and mentally. In both cases I lacked direction, I reacted to the fear, and I allowed the fear to get the best of me. Only until I acknowledged the fear and the truly underlying lack did a calming come over me to allow me to remember the advice from Imelda.

Notice the lack was still underneath the surface, showing itself to me in different ways, and trying to get my attention. Whatever is in lack will capture the attention of the individual (both consciously and/or unconsciously) causing a perpetual cycle until the lack was filled.

That job forced me to confront my lack state of being in the form of fear on a daily basis. It took more than six months to fully regain my state of confidence and trust within myself. Upon filling that lack from within there was no reason to stay so I quit the job the next day. Little did I know at the time, I still had more lack to deal with. It came in the form called "lack direction."

lack direction – (/lak də'rekSH(ə)n/noun)

1. to not know what you really want to do.

direction (/də'rekSH(ə)n/ noun)

1. a course along which someone or something moves.
2. the management or guidance of someone or something.

When you lack direction you are in a state of being without the proper guidance and/or to not know what you really want to do. You in essence lack the ability to take the right next step in the moment. In both cases, I was calling on Imelda for the next step to take in that moment in time. I was experiencing *lack of direction*!

It is critical to understand how it is very hard, if not impossible, to illicit a successful result if you don't know what you really want to experience. In essence, you lack the awareness of a successful aim, and that leads to the frustration and lack building from within until it leads you to experience a failure.

success (/sək'ses/noun)

1. the accomplishment of an aim or purpose.

The real problem is most people, me included, go through life never really getting all the right information they need to truly help when lack sets in. Why is that? Could there be something else going on still underneath the surface?

If failure precedes fear and lack precedes failure, then what precedes lack? The answer to this is the real truth behind lack. This is why we're shedding the light on fear, failure, and lack because all three conditions point to the underlying state we desire to be in at all times.

I felt like I won the lottery by taking Imelda's RICH Playbook course.[30] To live a rich life, we must be able to Reclaim our Integrity to Create Happiness. Look at the definition of happiness.

happiness (/ˈhapēnəs/noun)

1. the state of being happy.

Notice how the definition is similar to the lack definition but in lieu of "without," we replaced it with happy. Here lies the next question – both have the words "state of being" within them. Let's dig deeper at the definitions because they are leading us to the answer.

state (/stāt/noun)

1. the particular condition that someone or something is in at a specific time.
   a. a physical condition as regards internal or molecular form or structure.

being (/ˈbēiNG/noun)

1. existence.
2. the nature or essence of a person.

3. a real or imaginary living creature or entity, especially an intelligent one.

Another way of saying state of being is "someone of existence" and/or "someone of nature" who is intelligent. When we are happy, we are in a physical condition of existence on an internal and molecular form of feeling pleasure, contentment, fortunate, and even convenient! (see definition below)

happy (/ˈhapē/adjective)

1. feeling or showing pleasure or contentment.
   a. having a sense of confidence in or satisfaction with (a person, arrangement, or situation).
   b. satisfied with the quality or standard of.
   c. willing to do something.
   d. (of an event or situation) characterized by happiness.
   e. used in greetings.
2. fortunate and convenient.

Now let's keep bringing more information to light. What precedes state of being? The answer is in the definition of being which is "a real or imaginary living creature or entity, especially an intelligent one." The driving force behind all failure and all success is some type of higher intelligence.

Why is there a higher intelligence trying to get our attention? What is this higher intelligence? How does it fit into helping us understand the driving force behind all our good or bad decisions in life? Well, let's first understand what intelligence means.

intelligence (/inˈteləjəns/noun)

1. the ability to acquire and apply knowledge and skills.

Notice how in the definition of being it also states a "real or imaginary living creature or entity." We have come this far let's continue to go further into this.

entity (/ˈen(t)ədē/noun)

1. a thing with distinct and independent existence.

existence (/igˈzistəns/noun)

1. the fact or state of living or having objective reality.

Based on the actual definitions at the core of it all, we are intelligent beings who are both part of and independent of this higher intelligence with the ability to change our states of being which can be real or imaginary in nature. We are multidimensional!

multidimensional (/ˌməltēdəˈmen(t)SH(ə)n(ə)l /adjective)

1. of or involving several dimensions or aspects.

If you feel fear and experience failure or feel fortunate and experience success, the constant is we are both part of and independent of this higher intelligence with multiple aspects at play as well. This is where we must begin our quest to fully understand how to best utilize this higher ability, knowledge, and skills, so we can experience more of what we want going forward.

Years ago, when Imelda developed her MAGIC course, I never imagined it would lead me here to this connection point. Remember: MAGIC stands for "Multi-Dimensional

Alignment with God's Infinite Creation."[31] What is magic and God's infinite creation? How does this all tie together?

magic (/ˈmajik/noun)

1. the power of apparently influencing the course of events by using mysterious or supernatural forces.

God (/gäd/noun)

1. (in Christianity and other monotheistic religions) the creator and ruler of the universe and source of all moral authority; the supreme being.
2. (in certain other religions) a superhuman being or spirit worshiped as having power over nature or human fortunes; a deity.

infinite (/ˈinfənət/adjective)

1. limitless or endless in space, extent, or size; impossible to measure or calculate.

creation (/krēˈāSH(ə)n/noun)

1. the action or process of bringing something into existence.

MAGIC doesn't happen on the well-traveled path. That path is scattered with twists, turns, ups, downs, failures, and successes because each one of us has the ability to change our states of being which can be real or imaginary in nature. It's like alchemy.

alchemy (/ˈalkəmē/noun)

1. the medieval forerunner of chemistry, based on the supposed transformation of matter. It was concerned particularly with attempts to convert base metals into gold or to find a universal elixir.

   a. Similar: chemistry, magic, sorcery, witchcraft, enchantment.
2. a seemingly magical process of transformation, creation, or combination.

Notice the second definition, a seemingly magical process of transformation, creation, or combination! We have the ability to alchemize our state of being which in turn magically transforms and creates an experience in the current reality.

At some point in the process, you will finally remember you are already a master at doing this when it comes to aligning with God's infinite creation which we call life.

If you're experiencing a failure, that is a sign you're aligning with a state of being of what you ***don't*** want to experience. While experiencing a success means you're aligning with a state of being of something you ***do*** want to experience. ***Which is why we aim to master our ability to align with the right state of being!***

Aligning with higher intelligence (ability, knowledge, and skill) is when one masters both failure and success at the same time. How do we better align with this higher intelligence?

You must choose to learn more about the fundamental structures at play first to consciously become more aware as to align with this higher intelligence. It is in this alignment where success grows and lack dies. You must remove the lack to unlock the successful desires to come into the current reality.

Here is one of the major problems that is very challenging in our day and age. There is an abundance of information, tools, specialists, experts, coaches, gurus, channels, guides, trainers vying for our attention. The list goes on forever. You could go insane (my journey felt this way) trying to figure out how one must align with this higher intelligence on your own, especially if you're driven by fear, failure, or lack.

It is that drive, that state of being which will fuel either outcome in your experience. Until you get more information, it is really hard to find clarity. The only way to find clarity is by first understanding the challenges everyone faces in regard to aligning with this higher intelligence on a consistent basis. Then once you understand the process of transforming a failure into a success then you will know that it is a learnable skill that can be practiced and ultimately mastered!

Before we do that, let's quickly recap before we head to the next chapter.

- One must understand the what, why, and how as it relates to failure and the transformation of it into a success.
- Failure precedes fear and lack precedes failure.
- Higher Intelligence precedes both lack and happiness.
- When you "lack direction" you are in a state of being without the proper guidance and/or to not know what you really want to do.
- The definition of *unlack* means to remove lack.
- Must acknowledge and recognize the existence of a higher intelligence at play in our life.
- Only upon aligning with higher intelligence can we tap into the MAGIC. MAGIC – Multi-dimensional Alignment with God's Infinite Creation.
- Upon alignment with one's desired state of being is when one masters both failure and success.

- The process of transforming a failure into a success is a skill that everyone can choose to master.

Now we need to answer the question, "Who should you listen to" in the next chapter.

PART 2

What, Why, and How Failure Functions in Our Lives

CHAPTER 2

WHO DO YOU LISTEN TO?

"If you make listening and observation your occupation, you will gain much more than you can by talk."
—Robert Baden-Powell [32]

As I sat there, it dawned on me that the main topic in the room was all about failure. Some people mentioned it as a badge of honor, some as an acknowledgement, while others shied away from the topic all together.

I went from presentation to presentation during this amazing Startup Cincy Week (five full days) for entrepreneurs and small business owners.[33] The topic of failure kept coming up in every conversation. It seemed like everyone was talking about it no matter if they were young, old, experienced entrepreneurs, new entrepreneurs, funders, angel investors, consultants, vendors, speakers, CEOs, successful and not so accomplished, all were discussing this topic.

It was clear to me there was much more to failure, and this internal burning curiosity was going to lead me on a quest for the answer. Then it hit me: maybe there is a right way and a wrong way to deal with failure. How do you stop the momentum of failing?

Maybe there is a way to use these failures and actually turn them into positives—real-life success stories that would allow you to live a life worth living, a life of happiness and joy because that person is better equipped to deal with the failures.

The ability to flip the script on failure and use it as the building blocks to grow is what true artists are able to do. They showcase above average skills in their particular industry. This mastery sets them apart from the many people who flounder when it comes to all the ramifications one goes through when a failure occurs.

How should we view failure in our lives? What is the right way to go about it at home or at work? How should we talk about it amongst our peers, family, even our children? All of this kept going on in my mind because everywhere I went it kept coming up as a top of mind subject.

Over the years I have heard a lot of quotes that you want to fail forward fast. I started my google search for more information with that in mind. "Fail forward fast" is a popular phrase in business that basically means failure may be part of the process, but learn from it (fast), pick up the pieces, and move on.[34]

I went on to read articles and viewpoints about failure, and they were what I'd always expected from surface level.[35] The articles had more suggestions of what to do but nothing of substance. I did come across an article with Brene Brown about failing brilliantly.[36-37] She gave some great tips on failing as it relates to business. (1) Failure's another word for education. (2) It's ultimately all up to you, but you can't do it alone. (3) It's not always nice, but it's always necessary.

I even talked about my start-up week experience with my parents, and I was mulling over the idea of actually writing about this subject. My mother flat out said, "Why do you need to talk about failure so much?" I didn't say anything back to her right away because, frankly, I didn't have a good enough answer at the time other than a gut feeling that there was something more to this subject.

I went online and searched for books on failure. Some well-known authors had written about this like John Maxwell, Tim Tebow, Seth Godin, Jim Collins, etc. I sat there asking myself "Is this something that we need to talk about again?" [38-42]

Then I remembered a statement of Imelda's that always resonated with me. "MAGIC doesn't happen on the well-traveled path." My path, my journey, is not going to go down the traditional route. Others might have non-traditional routes in their careers and experiences, and they might connect differently with certain topics, especially when it comes to my specific viewpoint as it relates to the topic of failure.

Failure in my eyes is the byproduct of something much deeper going on under the surface. This is why I spent most, if not all, of my time focusing on industry experts, information, and publications in those specific areas to pull together an easy to understand nine-step process that anyone could follow to success.

I consistently implemented the very same techniques and information I'm about to share with you to bring forth the results for my very own eyes. Only upon seeing the success in my daily life experience did I feel comfortable in sharing this content with you.

This topic of failure and success is a personal journey that everyone goes through. The only real way to properly display the personal journey is by sharing with you my real-life experiences. These experiences are being shared to help you remember and connect the dots in your personal journey. Maybe they will offer a much deeper insight to how magical this life can be once we strip back the façade.

Who do you listen to? This is the first real problem when it comes to why failure occurs. When you are in the state of lack and if you allow that lack to take up the emotional and mental bandwidth of your cognitive functions, you are more inclined to make other poor decisions.

Take a second and consider who you listened to when you made your last major decision. Was it based on a short-term expectation? Was the proper due diligence done? Who did you seek out for advice in making the decision? Was that person or source the right one? Did you make an educated decision based on that advice, or did you override your internal gut feeling?

The first major problem is we seem to be listening to the wrong people and/or sources more often than not. If you want to learn how to invest your money properly, the person you might want to seek advice from is Warren Buffet and Charlie Munger of Berkshire Hathaway.[43-45] They have proven over 50+ years they not only know how to invest money, they have physically shown the proven results of it.

Who do Warren and Charlie listen to when making a financial decision? These two quotes give you a very good insight.

"No," Warren says. "We don't read other people's opinions. We want to get the facts, and then think." And when it gets to the thinking part, for Buffett and Munger, there's no one better to think with than their partners. "Charlie can't encounter a problem without thinking of an answer," Warren says. "He has the best thirty-second mind I've ever seen. I'll call him up, and within thirty seconds, he'll grasp it. He sees things immediately." [46]

It's interesting how Munger sees his ability to acquire knowledge as a learned skill rather than relying on natural ability.

"Neither Warren nor I is smart enough to make decisions with no time to think," Munger once told a reporter. "We make actual decisions very rapidly, but that's because we've spent so much time preparing ourselves by quietly sitting and reading and thinking." [47]

These two men spend over 80% of their time reading and thinking about what they read. This allows them the ability to pull from their inner knowledge to effectively make a decision and be able to articulate that understanding to someone else. If you can't help someone else understand, then you probably don't have a good grasp of it.

Munger and Buffet believe that "most people don't grab the right ideas or don't know what to do with them." You see, this makes more sense with the poverty study. When people aren't in a state of lack, they can make sound decisions. When they are in a state of lack, those decisions turn out poor.

Reading these quotes from Charlie and Warren demonstrates the real underlying problem that leads to that poor decision. It is not the money; it is the lack of access to the right information when a person is faced with a decision. Many times, decisions are made from the wrong perspective which leads to another wrong choice, which leads to another failure, and that leads us to another opportunity to get it right the next time.

This is what causes the biggest frustration with most individuals. It seems no matter what they do, they hit a roadblock, or something continues to plague them that they cannot overcome. This is because they fail to see the root cause of the problem. Have you ever heard of the Band-Aid approach? It's a short term and usually hasty decision that covers up the symptoms but does little or nothing to mitigate the underlying problem.

Whatever challenges you're currently facing, (personal, business, relationships, health, money, etc.) they are all the symptoms of one specific root cause. You might be able to overcome some challenges, but until you address the root cause, you will most likely end up on the wrong side of success over the course of time. Let me tell you a quick story to better explain what I mean.

I was in the car with my mom. She likes to use a Garmin device as her GPS service.[48] Have you ever heard of Garmin? She has an older car and it's pretty easy for her to use. We set the Garmin, and she proceeded to drive to our end destination. As we were going along, the Garmin device wasn't in sync with the latest update. We came to our exit, but it was closed due to construction of the ramp.

This wouldn't have been a big deal any other time, but on this date, we were late for the FC Cincinnati soccer game.[49] Traffic was beginning to get backed up, and our major obstacle was lack of direction. I pulled out my phone and set the Waze app to our end destination.[50] It quickly calculated all the current traffic patterns and open exits to find us the fastest route to the stadium. It even told us the estimated time of arrival, which instantly put both of us at ease.

During this little transition, both the Garmin device and the Waze app were talking to us out load giving us two different directions as to the best route to take based on our current location and time schedule. Both would eventually get us to the end destination, but it was clear one service was much better equipped to handle the current circumstance than the other. Waze was able to get us to the game on time without the resistance as well.

Doesn't this example best explain what happens in real life? It begs the question of who should we listen to? Who has the right information particular to our specific needs at this very moment? When an unexpected roadblock pops up, you really don't have time to tell too many people your financial story or direction for the business. That might take too much time or, worse yet, forces you to take the long way around and have to experience the delays and circumstances associated with that decision.

Isn't it much easier to deal with one person than it is to deal with multiple people when it comes to most anything we do these days? But who is that One Person? This is where most people fail before they start. Most people seek information and advice for key decisions from individuals outside themselves. This, in my opinion, is equivalent to using the Band-Aid approach.

I know for a fact at this very moment, everyone already has the answers to every question, situation, or circumstance right within themselves. All they have to do is tap into their internal GPS system which is instantly equipped with all the updated current information. Who should you listen to? That's right. **You should listen to YOURSELF**! When you learn to trust and believe in yourself, it unlocks the infinite possibilities for you to find your path to success. This is what I mean by fixing the root cause!

Right here is where the opportunity and the challenge lie in most people. It's really hard to find a success to the failure with the same mindset that caused the failure in the first place . . . unless . . . you are able to plug into the awareness of someone who has a higher-domain awareness than you do.

This higher-domain awareness can be accessed in many ways. The most commonly used choice would be seeking advice from a wise person, a sage of some type, and/or get access to the information from an intuitive who can shed more light on the situation. Here is the major distinction: You're seeking a better advantage point to receive your information from an individual who has shown the ability to access this higher information.

Why do birds, like the eagle, osprey, and a hawk sit up in tall trees or buildings scoping out the scenery below? [51] They do it because they can survey and see their target from a mile away before taking flight toward it. These birds are accessing information from a better vantage point. If it started its search from the street level, the predator bird couldn't see the prey a mile away.

Plugging into the awareness allows you to tap into the MAGIC of someone else *while you re-align with your internal GPS system.* At some point in the process, when you've worked out enough thoughts and feelings of lack within yourself, you are able to navigate the path to success with a level of belief necessary to achieve the right end destination point you were seeking all along.

This advice comes with one caveat; make sure you pick the right advisor. It should be someone that is updated with as many aspects of your specific needs and wants going forward. Otherwise, they will do more harm than good, causing you to experience delays, which will cause you to start the failure cycle all over again.

Listen to the people who have done what you want to do. Listen to people who have what you want and who have the physical evidence that it works. Discern their opinions from the facts and form your perspective. Then you need to decide whether to shift some of your assumptions from this new knowledge you accumulated.

The Buffett and Munger story really hit home on why lack of knowledge is the first major problem with why failure occurs in lieu of success. We're operating daily with outdated information, thoughts, emotions, feelings, and beliefs. Only when you have access to the current information are you truly able to make a sound decision quickly and effectively.

The ability to access the right knowledge, when the time is right, seems to come much easier to those who have been able to quietly sit, think, and write out their perspective. How many people really take the time to do this?

Over the years, I have created a lot of business partnerships with a lot of different people. Most of them were in industries in which I had no real knowledge. I really didn't do any due diligence on the industry to better understand what was really going on. I was taking my partners words and insight at face value, never really taking the time to validate the information to be true for me.

Ultimately, many of these businesses never gained much traction because all the minds at the proverbial decision-making table were not operating at the same level of trust as Charlie and Warren. When you lack trust and a deep belief in your spouse, your employer, your product, your team, your business, or even yourself, that is where the failure sits.

In other words, everyone was failing because we were all taking cues from different GPS systems that were telling us the best route to take. None of them gave anyone the peace of mind that we would reach the destination. Who should you listen to? You should listen to yourself!

This is a daunting task in our current world, but I promise you, it can be done. As you go through the book, you will have all the information and techniques you need to be able to do that with complete trust. Have belief in yourself and that your natural gifts, talents, and abilities will guide you to the right next step to take.

Let's quickly recap before we address the next major challenge one must overcome to master failure and success.

- This topic of failure and success is a personal journey that everyone goes through.
- It is the lack of access to the right information when the decision needs to be made that causes most people to fail.
- Plug into the awareness of someone who has a higher-domain awareness than you do and who has already achieved the results you want to achieve, and then discern the facts and formulate the right decision for you.
- Who should you listen to? That's right you should listen to YOURSELF!
- Fix the root cause! When you learn to trust and believe in yourself, it unlocks the infinite possibilities for you to find your path to success.

This leads us to the next major obstacle of why failure is so prominent, and it comes in the form of teachability.

CHAPTER 3

THE INVISIBLE GLASS CEILING

"Failure is the mother of success."
—Chinese Proverb [52]

Life does not happen the way we envision it. I know that doesn't sound profound. We go through life with a vision of success, and sure enough, when we think we're going to obtain it, an unexpected failure pops up. One day after many years of failing, this led me to ask the question, "Why does this happen?"

The Chinese proverb above is a great way to get into this topic about failure and how to effectively use it to your advantage in life and in business going forward. I didn't wake up one day thinking about this failure topic in the least bit. There was an inner curiosity and fear that I was somehow the cause to why my life was turning out this way.

Life has been a whirlwind since I graduated from college in 2000. Nothing has turned out the way I'd always envisioned it would. I was going to live a life worth living with the money, the girl, the career, the perfect home, the time off, and the clout.

As I chased that lifestyle, there was something else going on underneath the surface causing me to make critical decisions that affected the way it turned out. It felt like, no matter what I did, I kept hitting an invisible glass ceiling, and as time went on, I began to become very jaded with the world. Why?

Even after I took Imelda's RICH Playbook course, answers to my most pressing questions wouldn't come into focus. I remember distinctly how I was feeling when I took her course that day. It was like the information was landing on me differently and with more context than before. I was open, I was willing, and I was conscious of every word I was reading, thinking, and writing. In other words, something was rising and beginning to transform inside of me.

It was like layers upon layers of my heart were healing and coming online at the same time. I never felt so invested, so in the present moment, and so connected to something bigger than myself. Then another thought popped into my head.

Why was I feeling this way then and not a year later? Why was I having this profound transformation at that exact moment and not now?

These answers eluded me until a year later when the timing was right to receive them. I came across this audio from Kevin Trudeau about the teachability index.[53] He was mentioning that the way he learned was through mentorship. He was first trained that you must be teachable.

"You must be teachable. Believe but question the teaching until it resonates to be true to you. The teachability index is a measure of your willingness to do two things. What is your willingness to learn and accept change? Meaning you must be able to give up your favorite thing. You must be willing to change the way you think, do, act and be willing to listen to a different point of view. Once you have a high willingness to learn and change, then you can become an apprentice to a mentor."

Your teachability index changes depending on how you're able to absorb and use the information.[54-57] It can change at a moment's notice. Therefore, it took me so long to get the answers to my questions from a year earlier. I was not able to absorb any more information at that time.

"TEACHABILITY INDEX"

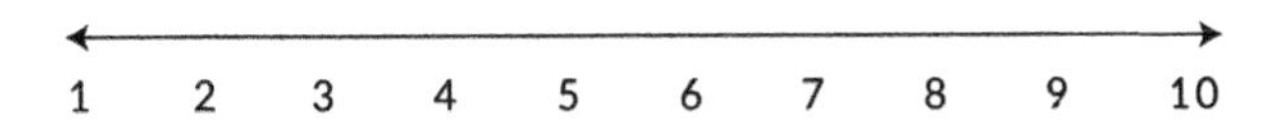

2. What is your willingness to change?

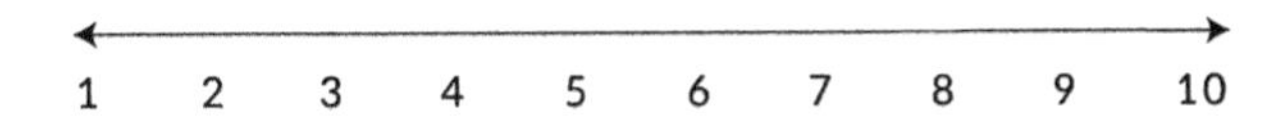

I had a high teachability index when I took Imelda's RICH playbook compared to my previous times taking it over the years. That is why it had such a profound effect on me at that moment. The minute I filled that void, the teachability index changed and so was my ability to learn and change as well.

This is what failure causes us to do. It allows us to become teachable again through showing us that the current way of doing things is not working to the expectation or success level intended. There is another way of going about it.

"We can't solve problems by using the same kind of thinking we used when we created them."
—Albert Einstein [58]

Until you're willing to make a change and think differently, you are physically and mentally unable to release the actual lack that is occurring. If your teachability index is so low, then you can only learn up to that level.

Warren and Charlie's teachability index must be pretty high because they are willing to absorb and use that information very effectively, compared to the teachability index level of the person who has money challenges and is unable to absorb and use that information very effectively. Our ability to be teachable directly affects our ability to deal with the failures that are occurring daily all around us.

My story about Imelda is very similar to many others as well. It's directly related to our willingness and ability to accept change. Often, we are not willing to change, and in fact, many of us view change as negative. Why is this?

Benjamin Kidd, who wrote The Science of Power, said, "Every person on earth is afraid of something. Most fears are inherited. In this essay, you may study the six basic fears which do the most damage. Your fears must be mastered before you can win in any worthwhile undertaking in life. Find out how many of the six fears are bothering you, but more important than this, determine, also how to conquer these fears." [59]

The Six Specters are labeled: Fear of Poverty, Fear of Death, Fear of Ill-Health, Fear of the Loss of Love, Fear of Old Age, and Fear of Criticism. The point is that fear is not the root cause that is the byproduct of something deeper going on. The clue is ***most fears are inherited***.

We are conditioned mentally, emotionally, and spiritually from the day we are born to inherently react to our daily interactions with life. Notice the word react. Often, we are reacting to what life brings us, and that is in direct opposition to being teachable where it calls forth our ability to be willing to change.

Many times we're too busy or under too much stress to have the presence of mind of not being in a teachable state. Usually, it takes a major event in our life to wake us up to the fact that we need to change something for a new outcome.

I was about 40 pounds overweight when Imelda passed. I didn't like what I saw in the mirror. I was a shell of the man I once was physically, and frankly, I got to the point that I needed to find a solution to regain my self-esteem. I was on the computer, and I saw this ad, so I clicked on it.

It was a program called "Get Lean in 12" by Karen and Shaun Hadsall.[60] He designed the program for people over 40. When you get older, your body, workouts, and food regime need to change because your body reacts differently as it did when we were in our 20s and 30s.

I purchased his program and followed it to a tee. I did every workout, I ate the foods, I documented my results in a notebook, and most importantly, I was in a very teachable state.

I had a high willingness to learn and accept a change in my life. I had no choice in the matter if I was going to live a rich life and be happy. I needed to be able to look in the mirror and say to myself, "I love you Brian." Within four months, I was down 40 pounds. For the next couple of years, I would fluctuate up and down. I didn't know why until I came across Chris Duncan, the CEO of The Conscious Education Company,

Founder of The Magnetic Mind Method, and Author of You're Not Broken.[61]

Chris did a webinar and he mentioned something in the webinar that helped add more clarity to this invisible glass ceiling. He mentioned that in our society there is an underlying energetic structure that is completely hindering our ability to sustain success for extended periods of time.

It is called the Problem Structure and it was discovered by Robert Fritz who is the author of the Path of Least Resistance.[62] His work for over 30+ years has been about how energetic structures affect our ability in both life and business.

So, I watched a couple of Robert's videos. In one of them he said, "The underlying structure of anything will determine its behavior. Most people don't think structurally; they think situationally. You can get rid of all of your problems and still not get what you want! Problem solving is not creating and creating is not problem solving."

Every one of our personal, family, and organizational behaviors is determined by the underlying structure of what created it. Once you consciously realize this, it allows you to take a step back from trying to solve the problem and instead choose to create.

Have you ever heard of the yo-yo effect? This is when you constantly fluctuate between what you're trying to experience and where you currently are today. It seems whenever you get close to what you want, something seems to happen to pull you back to where you started in the first place. That something is the underlying structure that's in place, keeping you within the structure's original framework.

Failures occur because our expectation is in direct violation of the underlying structure's capabilities for it to come into fruition. This can be incredibly frustrating because it seems no matter what you do, you can't get over the proverbial bump in the road. You begin to think short term or situational which further entrenches you to figure out a solution to the problem. This choice perpetuates the problem structure going on in today's society.

This is why it is so difficult to create change and maintain it because we begin the change with a false premise that was destined to fail from the beginning. The only way to break free from this problem structure is to *create a new structure not tied to the problem in the first place.*

IN THE PROBLEM STRUCTURE

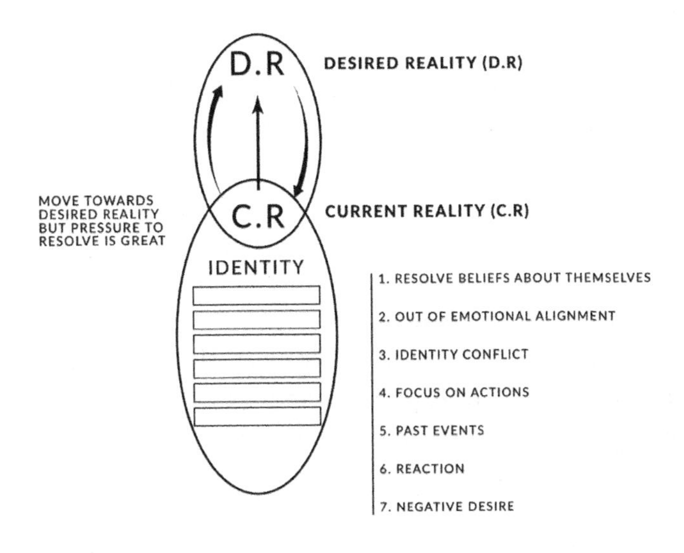

An example of this would be my fluctuating weight. The driving force behind getting the program was to lose weight and get lean. I was already approaching the situation that I had a weight problem.

No matter how much I followed the program, the tension would eventually become so great, and I would resort back to my original eating habits because that was the path of least resistance for the underlying energetic structure to release its tension.

I followed the program to a tee for four months and was able to lose 40 pounds. Then real life took over. I took a job that didn't allow me to follow the eating regimen and the work-out regimen like before. Pretty soon, I began to justify that it was okay to change back to my old way of eating. I was in better shape than before, but I was beginning to gain the weight back. I would fluctuate 20 pounds up or down over the next 2-3 years.

I would gain weight and then I would go really strict with my eating until I lost the weight again. The same thing would happen over and over. The reason was I always approached the situation from the same premise and point of view that I had a weight problem. I needed to find a solution to fix my weight problem permanently.

I made a subtle tweak to my underlying structure when it came to my health. I decided to simply choose to be healthy, vital, and fit. Notice how this choice has nothing to do with the problem? It simply has to do with the end destination point that I desire to experience more often. This tweak has allowed me to create a new underlying structure that better suits me in *obtaining and keeping* my end destination point.

When I align with my end destination point and raise my desire to transform through positive inspired actions, it provides me a better chance of choosing healthier food decisions, more consistent workouts, stretching, and food planning that better suits my lifestyle. These daily choices are better than what they were in the past, and my peace of mind is much better as well. I'm making healthier choices without the common self-inner talk that would have gone on without this distinct subtle change in structure.

The same is true for business and organizations. When I was a manager for a merchant services company, they had an underlying structure that led to burnout. The demand on the manager to perform many different aspects correctly on a daily basis was so great. If you or your team didn't meet the demands, the pressure would build exponentially.

The first couple underlying structures were the daily responsibilities and pay structure of the sales representatives of the team. It was very challenging to recruit and retain a quality salesperson with the company because of the learning curve in conjunction with the compensation constraints.

We had to make 100 phone calls (no purchased leads and no auto-dialer) in a three-hour span in the morning with the goal of setting two qualified appointments. Then we would go out on those appointments in the afternoon. In between those appointments, we needed to visit 25 businesses so we could continue to set more qualified appointments.

If our team didn't make enough phone calls (regardless of our total number of appointments set) that day, the pressure trickled down from the VP to the territory manager, then from the territory manager to me, and from me to the sales team. If the sales team didn't make enough phone calls, the territory manager made me do the calls in the evening just to put calls on the board so the VP would take the pressure off of him. Most business owners weren't picking up the phone after standard business hours, so these phone calls were not as effective.

This, in conjunction with multiple competing underlying structures of the position led to late evenings, not enough rest, not enough exercise, less time with Imelda, and higher turnover of sales reps due to the compensation and workday structure which in turn led to more pressure from the VP to the territory manager to the district manager to the sales team. Sure enough, after about one and half years of being a district manager, I left because of burnout. In reality, there was no way for me to thrive in that environment because the underlying structure of the position was too much.

The turnover of those manager positions to this day are still about one to two years or less. The turnover of sales reps are less than one to two weeks. Until they address the underlying structure there will be more of the same turnover regardless of who fills the positions. The underlying structure of anything will determine its behavior.

What are your underlying structures at this very moment? Are you experiencing yo-yo effects in multiple areas of your life? What is your teachability index at this very moment? Are you still willing to learn and accept a change in perspective about failure and success?

Therefore, when we re-read a book a year later, it lands on us differently than the year before because we truly are a different person than we were a year ago. The same was true when I took Imelda's course, and the same was true when I took Shaun's program, the merchant services job, and ultimately when failure shows up in our life.

The invisible glass ceiling that holds us back is both the underlying structures in conjunction with ourselves not being in a teachable state. When we are in a non-teachable state, we listen to the wrong people or fail to take the time necessary to be able to discern the information when the opportunity presents itself to us.

When we lack information, we seem to become stuck in our ways until an event comes along to shake us out of the usual way of doing things. In most cases, it has to do with some type of fear program running deep in our thoughts, emotions, and feelings.

A natural byproduct of mastering the basics laid out in this book is the ability to address fear and lack at a root level. In turn, this process allows you the ability to naturally reconnect with your internal guidance system and become teachable again without some traumatic event pushing you forward. When you become teachable, you can change, and when you change, so does your way of thinking, and ultimately, your behavior.

Soon, you will be able to uncover all fears and structures, known and unknown, to free yourself from the inherent bondage of the past, present, and future. At the same time, it will allow you to open your bandwidth to receive and become inspired so you can be proactive toward change.

Let's quickly recap this chapter for your notes:

- Once you have a high willingness to learn and change, you can become teachable.
- Failure allows us to become teachable again.
- There is a problem structure that holds us in a perpetual cycle of not creating.
- Problem solving is not creating and creating is not problem solving.
- The underlying structure of anything will determine its behavior.

- The invisible glass ceiling that holds us back is both the underlying structures in conjunction with ourselves not being in a teachable state as well.
- Once you address the lack at a root level, it frees you up to become teachable without the traumatic event to push you to change.
- When you become teachable, you can change, and when you change, so does your way of thinking and ultimately your behaviors.

This leads us to the next failure obstacles that affect who we listen to and our teachability index. It's the dilemma of the percentages between thoughts and actions.

CHAPTER 4

THE DILEMMA OF PERCENTAGES

"The ability to ask the right question is more than half the battle of finding the answer."
—Thomas J. Watson [63]

I began to write the outline, and still I felt reservations about this topic because something wasn't clicking in my mind. I have dealt with failure in my life, and as I thought back about all those failures, I don't think it dawned on me how much they affected the trajectory of my life.

It's not like every day you sit there and think about all your failures in life, right? From the amount of money I had lost in making bad business decisions, to the times I missed with Imelda from working too late, to the bad health choices I was making by eating the wrong foods, not exercising regularly, not speaking my mind enough, and the list continues. There was something more to this failure thing that wasn't making sense to me.

As I looked at my failures, it kept compounding how many of them were happening in many areas of my life. Usually when I failed at one thing, it translated over to another area then another. One bad decision based on a failure led to another bad decision which continued the cycle of failure. Then it dawned on me—maybe I'm going about this all wrong. Maybe I'm asking the wrong question. Instead of asking, "why should I talk about failure?" I should be asking, "what causes us to fail and how can that help me succeed?"

As a society, we fail every day of our lives in many areas. You failed to exercise because you were too busy with work. You failed to put down your phone at the dinner table to be present with your spouse. You failed to call your Mom to wish her a happy birthday. You failed to stand up for yourself in getting a promotion you deserved this year as it was promised. You failed to speak up for a friend who was being talked about in the wrong light . . . I think you get my point.

These failures are happening at a rapid rate, and they are happening to everyone around us 24/7/365, and not many people stop to ask what really causes us to fail.

I'm not talking about the superficial answers like we ran out of money, or my relationship failed because I was working too much. I'm talking about finding out the root cause, the underneath situation, the original feeling behind the failure. Are we in full control of our experiences?

I didn't know what I was looking for originally, and as I got more into this topic, it kept leading down a path that kept satisfying my inner quest for knowledge. What really causes us to fail? I knew I needed more research, and my first thought was Law of Attraction.[64-65]

The law of attraction is the attractive, magnetic power of the universe that draws similar energies together. It manifests through the power of creation, everywhere and in many ways.

Even the law of gravity is part of the law of attraction. This law attracts thoughts, ideas, people, situations, and circumstances.

I believe in the law of attraction, but if that is truly what is going on, then I am the one attracting these failures to myself. That is very disconcerting, to say the least. All these failures are because I'm attracting them to me. If that is the case, then I need to get to the bottom of this quickly to turn it around!

It was time to do some more scientific research on the law of attraction, and somehow, I got into this article about quantum physics and John Wheeler.[66] What came out of it was fascinating to say the least.

John Archibald Wheeler was a scientist and dreamer, colleague of Albert Einstein and Niels Bohr, mentor to many of today's leading physicists, and the man who chose the name "black hole" to describe the unimaginably dense, light-trapping objects now thought to be common throughout the universe. [67-69]

For the past two decades, he has pursued a far more provocative idea, something he calls genesis by observership. Our observations, he suggests, might contribute to the creation of physical reality. To Wheeler, we are not simply bystanders on a cosmic stage; we are shapers and creators living in a participatory universe. Isn't this another way of saying alchemy?

alchemy (/ˈalkəmē/noun)

1. the medieval forerunner of chemistry, based on the supposed transformation of matter. It was concerned particularly with attempts to convert base metals into gold or to find a universal elixir.
    a. Similar: chemistry, magic, sorcery, witchcraft, enchantment

2. a seemingly magical process of transformation, creation, or combination.

John feels our observation of any situation seems to shape our physical reality. If failure is as common as I think it is, this seems to confirm we are in some way causing ourselves to fail even if we don't mean to do it. In this same article, another bright mind seemed to weigh in on the subject.

Stanford University physicist Andrei Linde believes this quantum paradox gets to the heart of Wheeler's idea about the nature of the universe: The principles of quantum mechanics dictate severe limits on the certainty of our knowledge.[70]

"You know, if you say that we're smart enough to figure everything out, that is a very arrogant thought. If you say that we're not smart enough, that is a very humiliating thought. I come from Russia, where there is a fairy tale about two frogs in a can of sour cream. The frogs were drowning in the cream. There was nothing solid there; they could not jump from the can. One of the frogs understood there was no hope, and he stopped beating the sour cream with his legs. He died. He drowned in sour cream. The other one did not want to give up. There was absolutely no way it could change anything, but it kept kicking and kicking and kicking. And then all of a sudden, the sour cream was churned into butter. Then the frog stood on the butter and jumped out of the can. So, you look at the sour cream and you think, 'There is no way I can do anything with that.' But sometimes, unexpected things happen," according to Andrei Linde.

Now I feel really good that I'm finally asking the right question that should lead me in the right direction to the answer. By the genesis of observership, I'm going to choose to get to the root cause of what is really causing us/me to fail so I can ultimately figure out how to succeed.

No better way to start than with an observation from my past. I went for a stretch where every partnership in my business ventures went south. Unbelievable stuff was going on in and around me: vendors not honoring agreements, partners not doing what they promised to do, partners taking unauthorized money out of the business banking accounts, attorneys were involved, and many friendships were tarnished over this stretch.

As I sat in silence and thought about each venture, I realized I was the central piece to the puzzle. After the first failed business partnership, I went into the next one worried about the past experience of getting screwed over by my partners. There always seemed to be an uneasy feeling that one or multiple people were going to do something stupid to screw up the deal in some way. I would even talk about it with Imelda and do my best not to make the same mistakes I had made in a prior partnership. Regardless of the preparation, it kept on happening.

By the law of attraction and the Wheeler genesis of observership, I was attracting these failures into my physical existence. My thoughts were becoming things.

"We become what we think about most of the time, and that's the strangest secret."
—Earl Nightingale [71]

In hindsight, I was creating a self-fulfilling prophecy of the failure of the business without knowing it. I was thinking fear and worry, and when you do that, you attract the people, circumstances, and situations that match the vibration you are tuned into.

As a result, I didn't want to get into partnerships in business unless it was with someone like Imelda. That is what I have stuck to for the past couple of years. Since Imelda's passing, I have been offered a partnership or two and have reluctantly turned them down. I didn't want to go down the business partner failure route again unless the partner was aware of who they really are on a deeper level, and I was ready for a partnership.

When you find someone who is conscious of the way they are feeling, and they can adjust their internal feelings at any moment, you take notice of this ability. These types of people are a true reflection of what is possible for yourself when you decide to begin to master your innate skillset.

I'm not talking about skills in selling, management, relationships, business etc. I'm talking about your personal feelings and emotional intelligence skillset; the ability to know how you are feeling at the particular moment and adjust your feelings to go in the direction you desire. In other words, you can navigate yourself to a feeling of what you want to experience no matter what is going on in your life at the moment.

Also, you are conscious of how your decisions will affect the other person you are with. This could be your spouse, significant other, co-worker, children, family, or business partner. This consciousness level is always where I want to be, and I want to attract people who emulate the same conscious level going forward in my life.

In my earlier years, I thought it was the material things that mattered such as the house, the car, the money in the bank, etc. Those things still matter, but I was leaving out the other side of the equation: how I feel about my life as it is unfolding around me daily.

Originally, I was asking the question, "What do I need to do to make more money in my life?" I can see now that was the wrong question to ask. I should have asked the questions, "What am I doing that is causing me to experience this circumstance? What was I feeling when the unwanted circumstance was occurring in my life? How can I change my feeling, so this doesn't happen again in my life?"

This self-reflection on every circumstance has helped me to improve significantly in many areas. I'll give an example as it relates to work. Remember, I was selling financial merchant services to business owners, and it became apparent that this type of sale was truly a one-call close. Because of the circumstances of this financial service, the time constraint, and the effort involved, you needed to obtain a new client the very first time you met the individual in person, or your percentages of closing went down exponentially. This meant everything was important and needed to be scrutinized to get good at this on a regular basis.

When I didn't get a sale, I would take about five to ten minutes to silently reflect on the conversation and think about where I lost the deal. What did I say that I shouldn't have? What could I have said better? When was the perfect time to say that in the presentation? Did I use the right tone of voice? How did I feel when the objection came up? Did I have trouble communicating my point of view and confused them?

I revisited the conversation and pinpointed the exact spot I felt I lost the sale. I took a second to practice the right way to go about it going forward. This exercise got me to the point where I was closing well above the industry average! All because I took the time to ask the right questions, observe the past scenario, and pinpoint the root cause of the outcome I was experiencing.

Now that I think about it, this exercise was preparing me for this time in my life to be able to connect the dots and realize that it's important to ask the right questions in any situation. It's the questions that help you uncover the answers to the failure you're experiencing.

Back to this observership and thought concept. There is more to this than meets the eye. I was watching a video by Gregg Braden called *Living in a Reflected Reality.*[72] He mentioned we encounter three types of mirrors each day.

The first one is the *mirror of the moment, which means your life reflects to you what you see and feel.* This one is the simplest to understand. If you observe life as lack, you get more failures reflected back to you.

The second is the *mirror of that which is judged, which means the things that we judge will present itself over and over again, until we realize that it will keep happening again and again until we understand it is the charge we are placing on the people, situations, words, etc.* This is the mirror most people have the most trouble with. If you have a very strong judgement about integrity and always doing the right thing when someone isn't looking, then the other person might do something that showcases to you the direct opposite of that judgment by stealing money or cheating on you. Only when you get to a place of non-judgement on integrity will you lessen the charge. This mirror is all about allowing within another possibility of thought, action and feeling that you do not allow within yourself.

The third is the *mirror of relationships, what we have lost, have given away, or what has been taken away.* For example, there are times we are attracted to another person. You walk into a room and immediately you can't help but gravitate toward this individual. This mirror will give us insight into the pieces of ourselves we have given away or have been taken away, and you are attracted to this person to find those pieces again to become complete.

When I heard about the three mirrors and took the time to think about my past relationships, it all made more sense. These failures in the business deals were trying to get my attention so I could better observe my thoughts, judgements, emotions, and feelings. They were trying to get me to wake up, and each one was a different mirror reflecting back to me that information.

What happens if you have a group of people who are observing a situation? Does that collective focus help as well?

I remember a conversation with my Aunt Rita about the Heart Math Institute. They came across a study of a group of people who meditated for peace, and it had a direct correlation for decreasing murders and crimes in high areas. I searched for some scientific research, and I came across the Global Union for Scientists of Peace.[73-75]

Right on their website under the tab, scientific research, it states the following: "The unique effectiveness of the Brain-Based Approach to Peace in preventing social violence, terrorism, and war has been confirmed by more than 50 demonstrations and 23 scientific studies. This research has been carefully scrutinized by independent scholars and accepted for publication in leading, peer-reviewed academic journals. In every case, this approach produced marked reductions of crime, social violence, terrorism, and war, and increased peace and positivity in society."

I'm not going to go into all the details of the studies, so please reference the notes section for them. In basic terms, if a group of people observe a situation like war or crime in a specific area, they can decrease the situation by over 70% through a brain-based approach to peace! That is astounding to say the least.

Could we apply this methodology of observership to natural disasters, the economy, the success of a start-up company, and even a prosperous future for a family? Based on everything we know at this point; the answer is yes.

Our thoughts are becoming reality in our lives. The dilemma of the percentages is this: the more you think about what you don't want, the more you will get that reflected back to you in your reality. The more conscious you are of your thoughts and how you feel about them, the more aware of them you will become.

This is a major reason why I had so many problems over the years. I was focusing on the wrong things, thinking I was focusing on the right things. This is what causes the frustration, and that frustration triggers the inherit fears. The inherit fears trigger us to focus on the wrong things with greater intensity. That will initiate a failure to be reflected on us by one of the three mirror types.

Based on what we know so far, we must deal with lack at the root cause level. It's very hard to do because we must become teachable. We want to seek a solution, but for some reason, we keep focusing on the problem. This attracts another problem through the constant observership of the situation at hand and the underlying structure. Now the perpetual cycle of failure continues.

Knowing there is a cycle of failure allows you the opportunity to change your path at any time toward success. This is the foundational information you must know about for us to fill the lack of knowledge void from within. Once you assimilate the knowledge, it allows you to really move through the process much more quickly.

Let's quickly recap before we head to the next chapter:

- Our observations contribute to the creation of physical reality.
- We become what we think about most of the time. If we think of success, success will be reflected back. The same is true for failure.
- If you're not experiencing success then that means there is an underlying structure contradicting your conscious thoughts.
- Through our daily interactions, people, circumstances, and situations will reflect information that one must observe.
- Scientific research and studies have concluded that our positive observership can affect others in a positive way.
- The more conscious you are of your thoughts and how you feel about them, the more aware of them you will become.

Once we go through the nine-step process of failure and success, you will be able to recognize what to do when these types of people, circumstances, and situations show up in your life. Better yet, you will look forward to it! Plus, you'll be able to handle more happiness as it relates to your livelihood, abundance, health, relationships, and appearance.

CHAPTER 5

THE KEY TO FIGURING IT ALL OUT

"Devotion is the superpower that sustains the rigorous challenge. It is the light in your corner that fuels your endurance to go the distance."

—Imelda Arcilla [76]

In the NFL, many coaches and general managers seem to always state the following when doing interviews, "I want my players to be able to play fast.[77] I want them to fly around and stop thinking and naturally allow their abilities to be showcased in its fullest way."

In the NFL, they have an understanding that the biggest jump of productivity in a player is between their first and second year of playing in the league. The reason is the game has slowed down for the player, and they have been able to reflect on what areas they need to work on to become a better player.

This is no different for you and me as it relates to our livelihood in the workplace or if we own a business. The key to figuring it all out is you must get to a certain level of competence in order for this to happen.

Unfortunately, the biggest obstacle in our ability to experience more success is when you don't know that you don't know.

Ultimately, this is why I felt it is vital for you to get this information. Once you do understand it, you are no longer unconsciously incompetent on this subject.

You have the ability to become conscious to what is actually going on and are able to form your perspective on what you do know. To better understand this, we need to quickly go over the levels of competence. There are four steps you go through when processing information provided by Kevin Trudeau.[78-80]

Step 1: <u>Unconscious Incompetence:</u>

- When you don't know that you don't know.

Step 2: <u>Conscious Incompetence:</u>

- When you know that you don't know.

Step 3: <u>Conscious Competence:</u>

- When you know that you know.

Step 4: <u>Unconscious Competence:</u>

- You know, and it happens automatically.

An example of this is when you first learned how to drive to work. First, you put on the navigation system, and it leads you to the correct place. After driving to work over the course of time, you don't need to put on the navigation system at all.

You soon get to a point where you can be on the phone talking with a friend and still get to and from work safely. Ultimately, one day you will be deep in thought while driving, and time will fly by, and you will somehow get home. This is when you become unconsciously competent as it relates to driving to and from work. I feel most people, even myself, operate in the unconscious incompetence step more often than we should.

Larry Winget, an expert in personal development, has read over 5,000 books in his lifetime.[81] I was listening to him speak one time and he mentioned a couple of statistics as it relates to our reading habits that got me thinking.

According to Winget, to be considered an expert in any field, you must read around 500 books in and around that subject line. His point was it gives you the foundational information to pull from when it is needed. Based on researching how Charlie and Warren spend most of their time reading, I felt Larry was onto something, so I dug up some statistics to get better educated on the subject.

The Pew Research Center released their latest data on American reading habits, and the results show some interesting—and somewhat surprising—trends. Roughly 72% of American adults read a book in 2015, continuing a gradual decline over the last five years (from 79% in 2011). However, these stats include people who reported reading "one book . . . in part," so it's unclear how many made it all the way through.[82]

The average number of books each person read over the course of a year was 12 . . . but that number is inflated by the most avid readers. The most frequently reported number was four books per year. Of course, there's plenty of variation among demographics. Certain groups read more, or less, than the country as a whole.[83]

This puts in perspective that not many people are reading books, and even if they do read, they read only portions of the book. Another statistic does claim that more and more people are starting to listen to audio books, so at least we're moving in the right direction.

The reason I bring this up is that in order for us to become unconsciously competent in any given subject, we must be able to practice, read, think, research, sit, write, and listen to get to that level. I don't think we need to read 500 books to become unconsciously competent in a particular subject line.

Malcom Gladwell's *Outliers,* which repeatedly mentions the "10,000-Hour Rule," claiming the key to achieving world-class expertise in any skill is, to a large extent, a matter of practicing the correct way for a total of around 10,000 hours.[84]

Now, 10,000 hours of doing something is a lot. If you took practicing something one hour a day it would take a little over 27 years to become deemed an expert. That is some serious commitment to say the least. Not many people can be deemed world-class or an expert in anything. As you can see, it takes a lot of devotion to do anything at a high skill level.

It's clear we're not reading, thinking, and applying ourselves enough on different topics. This means for the most part, I and many others would be classified as unconsciously incompetent in those specific areas. Figuring this all out is key to finding your path to success.

Once you realize there is a process as it relates to processing information and to become skilled at something, it gives you physical proof that it is attainable. It doesn't have to take reading 500 books or 27+ years (doing something for one hour a day) to obtain the mastery of becoming unconsciously competent, it only takes devotion. Here is what Imelda said about this in a women's entrepreneur related interview she gave a couple of years ago: [85]

"It takes the devotion; meaning it takes consistency. It's devotion beyond the ordinary commitment. Devotion is the superpower that sustains the rigorous challenge. It is the light in your corner that fuels your endurance to go the distance. Why are you willing to dedicate your life force to alchemize your mind and transform it into a more evolved being time and time again? Because each cycle of growth you undertake is a bandwidth of potential to master your life and your business. To eventually create your life. So, the implications of that alone is breathtakingly open to the possibilities that you possess. Entrepreneurship is just the mechanism by which to really activate your own creator ability. So, when you are in harmony with your creator ability, your result is the desire that you're aiming for, whatever your dream is!"

This process works for any level of skill set you want to master as long as you're devoted to it. Look at the definition below.

devotion (/dəˈvōSH(ə)n/noun)

1. love, loyalty, or enthusiasm for a person, activity, or cause.
2. religious worship or observance.

First, notice the word observance. We learned how important observership is from the previous chapter to creating our current reality. Second, notice it states you must love, be loyal, or be enthused about a person, activity, or cause.

Here is one of the keys to figuring it all out, "can't we be devoted to an activity that we don't want?" Isn't that what lack is? The constant failures meant somewhere in my underlying structure I was unconsciously competent (actually deemed an expert) in lack!

It doesn't feel good to be an expert in failure but at least I'm now consciously aware of it so I can own it and choose to change it. The moment I take responsibility for it means I can now become more teachable in figuring out how to become unconsciously competent in success.

Your objective is to get to the unconscious competence level where the information you're pulling from is automatic, and in alignment with an inner knowing feeling of what you want to experience. It is in this automatic and inner knowing feeling where you become more confident in the task at hand with an inspired action.

That is why you become so much better at your job once you have been there for a while. You're not thinking about the how! You're taking the right steps without consciously thinking about it. This is why the NFL players get so much better from year one to year two because they are not consciously thinking, they are unconsciously competently thinking.

This is when the magic starts to happen with whatever you are focusing your thoughts and feelings toward. If you are not experiencing the success you want, and failure is showing up in your life, this is showing you on a competence level where you stand in that thought and feeling process.

I know what you're thinking – this is great Brian, but why is this the key to figuring it all out? Once you understand the way you magically process information, it allows you to begin to fully understand the path to your success when a situation surfaces.

You must master these concepts to the unconscious competence level because it is the foundation to everything else we will use going forward. Upon mastery of the basics, you can fully enjoy both your failures and successes that unfold within your experience. In fact, you will revel when something does go wrong because you know exactly what you need to do next in order to experience a better outcome next time around.

"Any man could, if he were so inclined, be the sculptor of his own brain."
—Santiago Ramon y Cajal [86]

If the goal is to become unconsciously competent in success, then we must understand the basics as to how information travels in our brain. It starts with the neuro pathways.[87]

The pathways along which information travels through the neurons (nerve cells) of the brain can be compared with the paths through a forest. As people keep taking the same route through a forest, they wear out a path in it. Every time you learn something, neural circuits are altered in your brain.

We recall what we learn when we continue to go over the same information until it is able to be recalled consciously and then ultimately unconsciously. If you are experiencing failures in your life, then there are neuropathways that have been created with some type of lack within them.

How does the conscious, subconscious, and unconscious mind work? [88] And what is the difference between them?

The unconscious constantly communicates with the conscious mind via our subconscious and is what provides us with the meaning to all our interactions with the world, filtered through your values, beliefs and habits. It communicates through feelings, emotions, imagination, sensations, and dreams.

A common way to illustrate the concept of the three minds is by using a triangle. Imagine at the very tip of the triangle is your conscious mind. It occupies only a small portion of space at the top, a bit like an iceberg where only a fraction of it is showing above the water. It probably represents about 10% of your brain capacity.

THE CONCEPT OF THE THREE MINDS

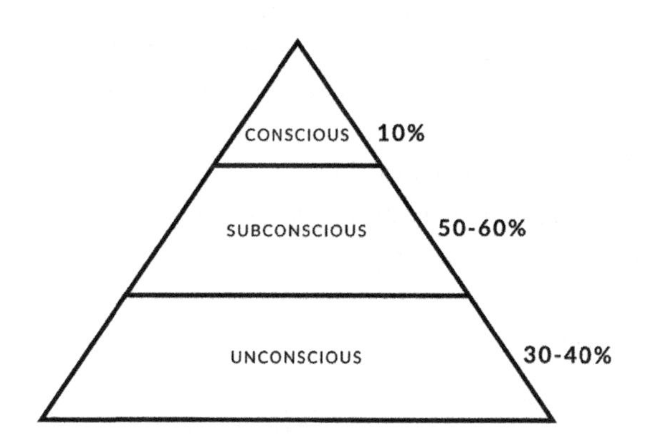

Below this is a slightly larger section that Sigmund Freud, an Austrian neurologist and one of the founders of psychoanalysis, called the preconscious, or what some refer to as the subconscious.[89] It is much larger than the conscious mind and accounts for around 50-60% of your brain capabilities.

The section below this is the unconscious mind. It occupies the whole width of the base of the triangle and fills out the other 30-40% of the triangle. It is vast and deep and largely inaccessible to conscious thought, a bit like the dark depths of the ocean.

Another common image is the iceberg where 5% of our conscious thoughts are above water and 95% of our subconscious thoughts are below the water.

As for the term "subconscious," Freud used it interchangeably with "unconscious" at the outset. The words are similarly close but not identical in German (subconscious is das Unterbewusste; unconscious is das Unbewusste). But he eventually stuck with the latter term to avoid confusion.[90]

According to the other well-known founder of psychoanalysis, Carl Jung, our unconscious mind is really expansive in nature.[91] His research shows that our unconscious mind holds repressed information of not only this lifetime but also our ancestral past as well.

Jung's notion of the collective (or transpersonal) unconscious is his most original and controversial contribution to personality theory.

This is a level of unconscious shared with other members of the human species comprising latent memories from our ancestral and evolutionary past. "The form of the world into which [a person] is born is already inborn in him, as a virtual image."

This distinction along with a couple of others showcase the differences between both Freud and Jung (as shown below). I personally side more with Carl Jung's perspective as you will see throughout the rest of the book, my actual experiences, and the research will show this as well. This information is vital, so you have a solid foundation going forward to pull from.[92]

DIFFERENCES BETWEEN JUNG AND FREUD

ASSUMPTION	JUNG	FREUD
Nature and purpose of the libido	A generalize source of psychic energy motivating a range of behaviors.	A source of psychic energy specific to sexual gratification.
Nature of the unconscious	A storehouse of repressed memories specific to the individual and our ancestral past.	A storehouse for unacceptable repressed desires specific to the individual.
Cause of behavior	Past experiences in addition to future aspiration.	Past experiences, particularly in childhood.

Our deepest memories and feelings are located in our unconscious mind. The subconscious uses these memories to explain, rationalize, and get the answers to our everyday questions we ask it.

We use our conscious mind to function each day, but only at a capacity of 1-5% of the time. 95-99% of our daily actions are being completed on autopilot by our subconscious and unconscious mind.[93]

Underneath the surface, our subconscious and unconscious mind is always running and thinking without the knowledge of our conscious mind. This is why you can think one way but not experience what you want to experience.

In 2005, the National Science Foundation published an article regarding research about human thoughts per day. The average person has about 12,000 to 60,000 thoughts per day. Of those, 95% are exactly the same repetitive thoughts as the day before and about 80% are negative.[94]

Bruce Lipton, well-known professor and scientist of the brain with over 40+ years of knowledge, lends some interesting facts on the situation as well.[95] Our perceptions and habits are formed through genetics and are learned at a very early age. From the day we are born to around six years old, our subconscious and unconscious minds have been programmed entirely by our environment, parents, and interactions to the world. Only when we get to around six do we begin to have the ability to consciously think.

Why is this important? Essentially, the studies show that almost 95-99% of our daily thoughts, emotions, and feelings are completed through the subconscious and unconscious mind. This unconscious mind was programmed during the first four-to-seven years of your life. This even includes the environment, thoughts, emotions, and feelings of the parents and anyone else that interacted with you during that stage.

If the other person (in this lifetime and/or including genetic ancestral past) felt lack in any way, that information was programmed into your unconscious mind. Remember, the unconscious mind is always thinking and running without the knowledge of the conscious mind. Hence the term unconscious.

This means we are unconsciously thinking most of the day! If you have positive thoughts, your life will reflect that back to you. If you have negative thoughts, your life will reflect that back to you as well. The key is to choose to program your mind to become unconsciously competent in the positive thoughts.

Only by creating more positive neuro pathways can you counteract the lack in the neuropathways that have become the major superhighways of your subconscious mind, which connects your unconscious mind to your conscious mind.

You have the ability to tell the subconscious mind what you want to think. Over time and through various methods of practice, you will be able to change the pool of feelings, emotions, imagination, sensations, and dreams that the unconscious mind uses to filter the beliefs and habits it pulls from to the conscious mind.

I didn't fully understand the relevance of this until I dug deeper into this subject line of the mind. This is the key focus area of all successful individuals—*they have mastered the way they think and feel.* This is the magic; this is the path less traveled on how you find your success. When your positive thoughts become more prominent than your negative thoughts through the unconscious mind, success becomes more prevalent in your life.

How long will it take to make this transition into more positive thoughts than negative? Phillippa Lally, a health psychology researcher at University College London, published a study in the European Journal of Social Psychology.[96] Lally and her research team decided to figure out how long it actually takes to form a habit. On average, it takes more than two months before a new behavior becomes automatic—66 days to be exact. How long it takes a new habit to form can vary widely depending on the behavior, the person, and the circumstances.

In Lally's study, it took anywhere from 18 days to 254 days for people to form a new habit.

As you can see, this provides much greater clarification on the timeline. It will take you on average from two to eight months to build a new behavior into your life. Herein lies the problem that most people fall into as it relates to changing our behaviors and habits. The time element is in direct proportion to your ability to harness the power of your conscious thoughts in conjunction with your inner beliefs.

Here is why there is such a wide range of time between the ability to form a new habit.

- Our conscious mind (5%) which we use to control our insights, reason, will power, motivation, and positive thinking only has the ability to illicit new neuropathways at a processing rate of a 40 BITs. (The definition of a bit is a basic unit of information in information theory, computing, and digital communications.) [97]
- Our subconscious and unconscious mind (95%) which controls everything else we do, think, act, feel, and say when we are not using our conscious mind has the processing rate of 40 Million BITs!

This is why, in a world of instant gratification, most people get discouraged before they have the ability to create new positive neuropathways. Their expectation is to quickly influence the unconscious mind with positive thinking alone, but as you can see, you're only working with a 40 BIT Processor!

Our subconscious and unconscious mind processing power is 40 Million times stronger, and if you have negative neuropathways running in the background influencing all your thoughts, emotions, and beliefs, that is where the problem lies. When I learned about this processing power of the subconscious, I immediately looked at this as a major positive because once you create some new powerful habits, the unconscious mind will quickly do all the work for you! [98]

Since we have around 60,000 thoughts each day and 95% of those thoughts are the same as yesterday, it wouldn't be much of a stretch to become a master of your thoughts in a short amount of time if we use this process of thought to our advantage.[99-100]

If the Shaolin Monk (as mentioned in the Introduction) is afraid of the man who has thrown one punch 10,000 times, then how long would it take for one positive thought to be repeated 10,000 times in our unconscious mind before we master it? Think about how powerful the unconscious mind truly is and how quickly it can be programmed to work for you instead of against you.

This is why it is very important to be conscious of your daily thoughts, emotions, feelings, and beliefs. They will literally trigger your subconscious and unconscious daily thoughts, emotions, feelings, and beliefs. When you're in a state of being of what you want, it allows the alignment to take place giving you access to the information you are seeking.

Notice how I say access because the information is going to come from somewhere as you go through your day in some way. You will get an intuitive hit, feelings, an inner knowing, or a flash that will allow you to access the information. Then you continue to follow the process until the success is realized.

When you master the basics, this information will flow to you naturally without having to think about it. It will become as natural as brushing your teeth. This is when the MAGIC happens effortlessly, and the successes continue to come on a daily basis. Even when you come across a minor setback, you won't see it that way. You will see it as a perfect opportunity to tweak the destination to make the next success even better than you imagined.

This is mastery of failure and success. It can only be obtained for those select few who choose to listen to their internal guidance system, begin to observe and interact with the world differently, and become very conscious of their teachability index. This is when their efforts and devotion to doing the daily actions necessary to reprogram the unconscious mind pays off.

The unconscious mind will do the heavy lifting when it comes to changing your experience! This is alchemy and the magical transformational process of creation. This is how you consciously create what you want.

Sounds kind of fun, doesn't it? Honestly, it is fun once you begin the daily activities if you go in with the mindset that every moment and in every way, my life keeps getting better and better! Every thought, every emotion, every feeling, and every belief gets a daily positive, energetic boost until the subconscious picks it up and continuously repeats the process unconsciously over and over again.

By changing some negative thoughts to positive thoughts, the power of the unconscious mind will take over. Let's say one positive thought a day is mastered consciously and then the unconscious mind takes over repeating that positive thought.[101]

One conscious hour of positive thought is compounding daily with the unconscious repeating it the rest of the day. This is reinforced again consciously for one hour the following day, then the unconscious mind will take over repeating it the rest of the day, etc.

Five hundred hours (correlation to 500 books need to be read in a subject line to become an expert) divided by 24 hours equals 20.83 days which, ironically, comes very close to the common saying about taking 21 days in a row to create a new habit.[102] This falls in line with Lally's study discussed earlier. Notice how this timeframe states creating a new habit is not mastery of the new habit. You still need to be diligent in your daily activities until the neuropathways grow to the point that the unconscious picks it up as a belief. This is the point of the process when mastery of that new habit is obtained.

Remember, this takes 18 to 254 days to create a new habit. This is where another challenge is largely misunderstood in our society of instant gratification. A lot of modalities such as hypnosis, affirmations, recodes, and some other practices will help speed up the reprogramming process but only with consistency.

If you have been thinking and feeling one way for 20, 30, or 40+ years, that is a very strong and secure neuropathway. You can instantly change and form a new thought or belief with a new neuropathway. But getting it to become strong and secure takes time and consistent practice. It takes devotion to sustain the rigorous challenge of 20, 30, or 40+ years of programming!

Now that you are consciously aware of this path to successfully create new positive neuropathways, you have a better chance of using it to become unconsciously competent. *All true change can only happen in the unconscious mind.*

Remember, the goal is to counteract enough negative thoughts until our overall daily thoughts are more positive than negative. It's very simple to understand on the surface, and it will become much easier to implement once you fully understand how to align, raise, and transform the failure into a success through the 9-step process we're about to explore in the next couple of chapters.

Let's recap the four major challenges that we need to address to truly fix the root cause of failure which is lack. Only when we *unlack* can we unlock more success to come into our life.

1. **Who Do You Listen To?:** You must begin to listen to your inner guidance system. Find people who have done what you want to do and do your best to mimic what they do while following your inner wisdom as the final decision maker.
2. **The Invisible Glass Ceiling:** We must become willing to learn and accept change without having to rely on a failure to occur in our lives to push us to the point of becoming teachable. Understand there are underlying energetic structures that dictate our behaviors. It is much easier to be proactive with our intentions than to be reactive to how life expresses itself to you each day. The daily activities we will soon discuss will naturally stimulate you to do this.
3. **The Dilemma of Percentages:** Whatever we observe most of the time, either negatively or positively, we attract into our lives. The failures are there to bring to light something within you that needs to be changed such as a thought, emotion, judgment, feeling, or a belief. Choose to ask the right questions to uncover the lesson and focus more on the positive

to better increase the percentages in your favor to experience more success.

4. **The Key to Figuring it All Out:** Now that we are consciously aware that our thoughts directly affect our behaviors and failures, we must choose to become unconsciously competent in the positive direction. All true change can only occur in the unconscious mind. It takes consistent thoughts and beliefs to influence the subconscious and unconscious mind which in turn directly influences our conscious behaviors. Once you create the new positive behavior and/or thought, the unconscious mind will do all the daily heavy lifting, ultimately changing your daily experiences.

Now you know what you need to focus on. To master failure and success, you must solve a root cause which is the lack within. Everything in your daily activities is designed to raise this balance of lack to the point where it tips toward the positive column and unlocks success.

Here are the quick notes from this chapter for review.

- The goal is to become unconsciously competent with your positive thoughts. Once you know, it happens automatically.
- Of course, we use our conscious mind to function every day but only at a capacity of one to five percent (1-5%) of the time. Ninety-five to ninety-nine percent (95-99%) of our daily actions are being completed on autopilot by our unconscious mind.
- As for the term "subconscious," Freud used it interchangeably with "unconscious" at the outset.

- Jung believes our unconscious mind is able to access other human species' thoughts and latent memories of our ancestral and evolutionary past.
- Our conscious mind (5%) which we use to control our insights, reason, willpower, motivation, and positive thinking only has the ability to illicit new neuropathways at a processing rate of 40 BITs.
- Our unconscious mind (95%) which controls everything else we do, think, act, feel, and say when we are not using our conscious mind, has the processing rate of 40 Million BITs.
- One (1) conscious hour of positive thought is compounding daily with the repeat thinking of it unconsciously the rest of the day. Reinforced again consciously for one hour the following day, the unconscious mind will take over, repeating it the rest of the day.
- All true change can only happen in the unconscious mind.
- It takes 18 to 254 days to create a new habit or behavior.
- Mastery of the positive thought only comes when the subconscious mind pulls the positive thought from the unconscious mind repeatedly without you consciously thinking about it. It will be expressed through your behavior.

When you choose to master the basics through the processes outlined in this book, the byproduct of doing so is immensely beneficial. You will be able to find your path to success with ease and grace, no matter the circumstances. You will have full control over your conscious and unconscious minds, emotions, and inner beliefs, and this will directly influence your behavior. Because you mastered these skillsets, you will be able to handle more happiness as it relates to your livelihood, abundance, health, relationships, and appearance.

This is truly on a soul level—what you have been seeking all along. MAGIC doesn't happen on the well-traveled path. To get you on that right path to success, MAGIC will constantly dangle a carrot in front of you to lead in the right direction of using your free will as you're about to learn in the next chapter.

PART 3

When Failure Shows Up You Need to Unlack

CHAPTER 6

THERE ARE NO MISTAKES

"It's not failure. It's actually being saved from an ordinary life!"
—Marilyn Jenquin [103]

I was about to finish up the book and turn it into the publisher when a thought (aka intuitive hit) popped into my head that I should check to see if Imelda was good to go with the book. I was meaning to connect with a medium and then out of the blue I noticed that I missed a phone call from Marilyn Jenquin of the International Foundation for Spiritual Knowledge (IFSK).

I called her back and she immediately apologized for dialing the wrong Brian and I cut her off immediately to schedule a medium reading to better connect with Imelda on this subject. Marilyn has done numerous readings over the years for me in connecting with Imelda after she passed and has been instrumental for me to gain better clarity from her as well. She did say something that caught my ear before she hung up the phone, "there are no mistakes."

Two days later we had our wonderful zoom call and Imelda was definitely present and in full force.[104] The first thing she stated through Marilyn was the number six. "Brian does the number six mean anything to you?" When she said six I knew she meant chapter six of the book. I guess Imelda felt this chapter needed to be tweaked a little bit better before it would get her final stamp of approval. (Let's see how I do!)

The point Imelda was trying to make was that we always have free will on what we get to choose to experience at any moment in time. To better understand her point let's start with the definition of free will below.

free will (noun)

1. The ability or discretion to choose; free choice.
2. The power of making choices that are neither determined by natural causality nor predestined by fate or divine will.

Boom! Look at the second meaning and I clearly understand what she was trying to get me to look at now. We have the power to make any choice neither determined by natural causality nor predestined.

We get to choose that we are the predominant creative force in our life. Also, at the same time we get to choose if our free will is determined by natural causality or predestined fate or divine will as well.

Both choices are valid and true depending on the experience. Both are available to you because we always have the power of free will. I knew this on one level, but this is a broader way of looking at the choice of lack or success in our lives.

What if we use free will to choose an end destination that was never meant for us to obtain in the first place because if we actually obtained it that would set us off our own unique path to success of what would truly give us fulfillment and purpose in our life?

There are no mistakes when it comes to what your soul truly wants to experience in this lifetime. Especially if you understand how free will works in conjunction with the soul. Let's first review the definition of the soul so we can get on the same page.

soul (/sōl/noun)

1. the spiritual or immaterial part of a human being or animal, regarded as immortal.
2. emotional or intellectual energy or intensity, especially as revealed in a work of art or an artistic performance.

Our soul ultimately has its own path of success that it desires to experience in this lifetime. As you can see in the definition it is our immaterial part of being human. If we don't know our soul's ultimate desire and/or end destination point then it is most likely that we will unconsciously or consciously choose the wrong paths which will trigger the failures to happen.

Only to be reminded through the failures that we have the ability to use free will to choose a new path. In that choice of experiencing a new path you will be continuously directed through the experiences of lack or success to recalibrate your choices until you ultimately align up with your soul's journey. When you align up with your soul's journey you will experience the feelings associated with fulfillment and purpose.

fulfillment (fu̇(l)-ˈfil-mənt/noun)

1. the act or process of fulfilling
2. the act or process of delivering a product (such as a publication) to a customer.

purpose (pər-pəs/noun)

1. something set up as an object or end to be attained : INTENTION.
2. a subject under discussion or an action in course of execution

At our soul level, this is where it wants our physical human experience to be in alignment and balance with it. It uses the underlying lack or success mechanism to drive us towards this realization as you're about to witness from these following experiences.

"Your soul evolves through entrepreneurship."
—Imelda Arcilla [105]

Years ago, on my journey, I had a dream to one day be really wealthy. I had it all figured out to be a millionaire before the age of 30, so I thought. I even bet my Uncle Steve, and I was supremely confident in my abilities. Little did I know, my first major business failure would come in my senior year of college.

My cousin, Bobby, who lived in LA, brought back to the Midwest numerous cans of Red Bull.[106-108] Red Bull was an upcoming energy drink company out of California. Bobby was mixing it with clear alcohol beverages like vodka, etc. We had a great time over the holiday break drinking these mixed drinks before we went out, giving us a good buzz, saving a little money, and more importantly, allowing us to keep a sharper and clearer mind throughout the night.

Bobby was generous enough to give me a couple of cans to take back to college at the University of Iowa.[109] I was a bartender at one of the biggest bars in the Big Ten.[110] I shared the drink with my boss. He loved it and asked me to find out where to get more. This is where the epic failure comes in.

For some reason, I got sidetracked with school, having fun, and college life. Another college acquaintance who bartended across the block also had other plans to hit it big early in life. Instead of going on spring break senior year, he wrote a business plan and sent it to Red Bull.

He was able to lock in the distribution rights to Iowa and parts of Illinois before our senior year ended. He became a millionaire that day, and I was left with the memory of my first business failure. Every time you drink a Red Bull think of yours truly.

This memory was also going on in my mindset when I quit my elevator and escalator job. Thank goodness I experienced this "supposed first business failure" and had this underlying lack driving me to utilize my free will to choose the next adventure my soul was desiring to experience.

If I hit big financially right out of college, I would have never taken the path I was on, to become the man I was meant to become, through my entrepreneurial journey. That first supposed business failure literally led me to meeting Imelda just four short years later. Thank you soul for that!

"It's not failure, it's a success when you miss out."
—Marilyn Jenquin [111]

That lack of financial success was always operating underneath the surface and kept dangling the carrot of me chasing the millionaire dream when I moved to South Florida. Then age 30 came, then 40, and I was nowhere close to that millionaire goal I set for myself.

There was failure, after failure, after failure. Maybe you can relate. When you go years on your journey, and you're not even close to hitting your mark, it can mess up your mindset a little. It is a classic case of the dangling carrot effect.

Imelda brought up this theory to me years ago. When you become an entrepreneur, it feels like the universe is always dangling a carrot leading you from one situation to the next.[112] Every pivot, change, set back, or failure is the universe dangling the carrot in front of you to move to the next place in your journey called life.

Imelda felt the carrot symbolized the wanting of something (in my case financial abundance), and it was always right there in front of me—so close yet so far away from actually obtaining it. This is my personal belief in how the soul puts you in situations that forces you to fail in that particular moment, allowing you the opportunity to grow from that actual experience. It does this until you realize how the universe operates through lack, and then this magical transformational process of free will gets really, really fun!

"Your soul evolves through lack."
—Brian Rassi [113]

This growth essentially becomes the new foundation to which you have now up-leveled into a better version of your previous self. You can't obtain your true desire until you become (state of being) the person who can truly handle that desire. The true driving impulse of the soul is to evolve and to expand. The growth can be proactive but, in most cases, it seems to be more of a reactive situation that comes from a failure (aka lack).

Remember the definition of failure so we can go into how the dangling carrot of the soul works in real life.

failure (fālyər/noun)

1. lack of success.
    a. Synonyms: lack of success, nonfulfillment, defeat, collapse, foundering, etc.
2. the omission of expected or required action.

The lack or success mechanism is in place to help guide us to what we truly want to experience. Something has to be the impetus for us to change and to become teachable. In most cases, something we don't want to happen actually begins to happen, and now you can catch it early and choose to redirect it toward a successful outcome.

Here is another example. I was growing a sales team with the hope of eventually being promoted, and I was knocking on the door of obtaining it. For reasons outside of my control, the office and work environment were too volatile to get over the hump. The number of retail stores we were supporting was dwindling because of outside circumstances beyond our control.

My team members were placed in stores that had no business having multiple people in them because the traffic was not sufficient. This meant the weakest team members, who needed more opportunities to succeed by sheer numbers, were getting half as much. This led to them not making money since they were on straight commissions. This led to a change in the office environment dynamics, and stress was building from within. When stress, fear, and frustration kick in, your team can be greatly affected. As team members left, I was faced with rebuilding again.

Who failed in this situation? Did the owner fail for not placing the right people in the right spots? Did our service provider fail by not suppling us with more stores to meet the team's production needs? Did I fail for not recognizing this faster? Did the weaker team members fail for not working harder at their craft to get placed into better stores? Did the leaders fail for not protecting the morale of the sales teams at all times? Did the recruiting team fail for not bringing in more talented team members? Or was it all of the above?

Failure was being used in all these cases to affect many people in the office. Over 30+ people were affected by these series of failures on multiple levels. Every one of us was directly or indirectly involved whether we knew it or not. Those compounding failures allowed me to move on from that position and to open up my own company. They allowed me the opportunity to formulate a better daily plan for success and actually implement it effectively.

Yes, I'm very thankful for those failures, and I'm very thankful for those lessons. Those sales skills, training skills, speaking skills, leadership skills, daily planning skills, and team building skills come in very handy when running my business. It built up confidence, trust, and most importantly belief in my skill set going forward.

This lack or success mechanism happens every day between yourself, your family, your work, your community, your industry, your country, your continent, the world, the galaxy, and even the universe.

Another example of the lack or success mechanism could be in the form of natural disasters. Do you remember Hurricane Katrina in 2005? [114] Hurricane Katrina made landfall on the Gulf Coast and generated a huge disaster. The storm flooded New Orleans, killed more than 1,800 people, and caused $100 billion in property damage. [115] It was devastating to the greater

New Orleans area. Do a simple google search of it, and you'll see multiple layers of failures going on.

Over 50 levees were compromised, which led to 80% of the flooding that occurred. The engineering of the area failed starting with the drains, pumping stations, and storm drains.[116-117] Many residents failed to leave the area ahead of time, putting them in harm's way. The local and national governments failed to express the danger involved and to evacuate the area properly. Failure in initiative, failure in confusion, failure to learn from Hurricane Pam, one year earlier, failure to communicate between agencies, supply failures, and failure in making decisions. Fraud and abuse of over a $1-2 billion in wasted taxpayer money, failure to respond in time, and the list of failures goes on and on.

Why did all of these failures happen at once? What was the main reason behind this storm? Was it a failure to take care of the environment, which some feel is causing global warming? Is it the conspiracy theories of the government using HAARP to manipulate weather storms as a weapon? [118] Was it failure of expectations of the entire country placing too much belief in our government to respond better than the private sector?

This natural disaster affected so many people. Businesses went under, and people had to move all over the country to find a new place to start over. These multiple layers of failures exposed flaws and created lessons for individuals, communities, businesses, agencies, city governments, state government, national government, and even international relationships. Did this not dangle the carrot of free will for millions of people to evolve and go in a new direction toward their future success?

The multidimensional lack or success mechanism seems to be working at all times and in all areas of our lives. I feel it will continue until the day we pass away from this life. These failures cause you individually, groups collectively, communities nationally, and even nations globally to do much required self-reflection if they wish to improve. Once the failure happens, it is exposed for all to see, and hopefully it will be addressed so it doesn't happen again while leading people toward a successful outcome.

This Jedi mind trick eluded me for years, but you don't have to wait anymore to figure it out. Now that you're aware of this cycle, it allows you to change your perspective on why failure occurs in your life. In basic terms, you can change your point of view to allow the unconscious fear and lack to dissipate.

It is the lack vibrating in your energetic field that causes you to continue to experience more lack scenarios. The key is acknowledging you are in lack without being afraid of this acknowledgement. Nothing bad is going to happen to you by doing this.

In fact, when you honor the benefit of that lack in your life and why it was created in the first place, you will realize it was there to help you in some way. Once you find out why, the resistance of the lack will dissipate so you can change your energetic vibration.

Maybe the lack was there to keep you safe and protected because you weren't ready for the new opportunity at that point in time. Maybe lack was there to show you where you need to focus your attention so you could become whole again in that area. It is like a spotlight being shown on that exact area you should address next to give you the most satisfaction in this very moment.

The minute you change the energetic vibration of your emotion from lack to satisfaction, the failure situations will not arise as much in your life. On the contrary, more successes will arise because the base emotion is that of satisfaction in lieu of the lack vibration.

A better way of explaining this is with the classic radio. When you tune into a certain FM station, let's say 98.1, you will end up with 80's rock music. If you switch the dial to a new FM station, 102.3, you will hear country music.[119]

This is the same way the universe feeds you situations, people, circumstances, and opportunities in the form of the channel you're tuned into. If you are tuned into the lack station on the radio dial, the universe will continue to feed back to you situations that are conducive to the lack. If you're tuned into the satisfaction station, the universe will continue to feed you the situations, people, and opportunities conducive to the more prosperous vibration.

This is why some people are doing really well in life and others are not. They have figured out how to get tuned into the station (state of being) and the universe keeps bringing more opportunities to experience that state of being. This means the state of wealth will bring more money, the state of happy will bring more happiness, state of being healthy will bring better health, and I think you get the point.

Another classic example of the dangle the carrot of free will point of view happens when people get fired from a job or suddenly let go. This happened to me a couple of times in my life and this next story is about my father.

He was getting up there in age with his career in the flooring industry. He was with his company for many years and was doing really well financially. The company decided they were going to change up the management structure which meant he was no longer needed in his position.

This is a common occurrence these days, especially as the dynamics change in the workplace. Dad was two to three years away from turning 70. He wanted to keep working to keep his mind sharp, but where do you find a job at that age that pays well? Where do you find a job that fits his skill set and with a company that respects his knowledge?

He began to look for a job and nothing really was panning out until one of his former co-workers called him when he heard through the grapevine that my dad was no longer working with the company. He wanted to reach out to see what Dad was doing, and the conversation took a turn for the better. He mentioned a position that would allow my dad to work in the same industry.

It would give him freedom to start a business, to work from home, to work on his own time when he wanted, allow him to write detailed reports to keep his mind sharp, allowed him to drive which he loves to do, make a really great steady income which he was looking for, and ultimately, this is the kicker, they didn't have a person available in his area of the country.

In basic terms, it was the perfect opportunity for him to transition into a new stage in his life. Obviously, Dad was aspiring to, and more importantly vibrating, for something more in his life even though he didn't know it at the time. Maybe when he sits down to read this portion of the book, he'll be able to pinpoint what he was thinking and feeling internally at that time in his life to figure out where the dangling carrot of the soul was leading him.

This is how the universe works. It uses your desires and then places the right people, circumstances, situations, and opportunities in front of you to step into and experience. Many times, that comes in the transformational phase of failure to lead you toward the success.

In Dad's case, the failure could be how the current management structure was performing for the company. That indirect failure led Dad to his much better career path at that time in his life. Not all failures have to be directly because of you. They can be caused by outside people or circumstances as well.

It's the dangling carrot of the soul by which the universe causes you to continue to figure out what you like and don't like, which fuels your conscious mind to stop and ask the question, why is this happening to me?

Why did I fail at this job? Why am I feeling this way? Why did she leave me? Why am I sick? Could it be that I'm tuned into the wrong radio station at the moment? What emotion am I feeling at the moment? What can I do to change that emotion for the better so I can change my radio channel from lack to satisfaction, and then from satisfaction to happiness?

A great book to read about this entire emotion and changing of the channel is *Ask and It Is Given: Learning to Manifest Your Desires*" by Esther and Jerry Hicks. [120] Esther has an amazing methodology of how to change your emotions and experience this deliberate creation with the universe. I highly suggest opening yourself up to her wisdom and using it in your life. See The Emotional Guidance Scale for more information.

THE EMOTIONAL GUIDANCE SCALE

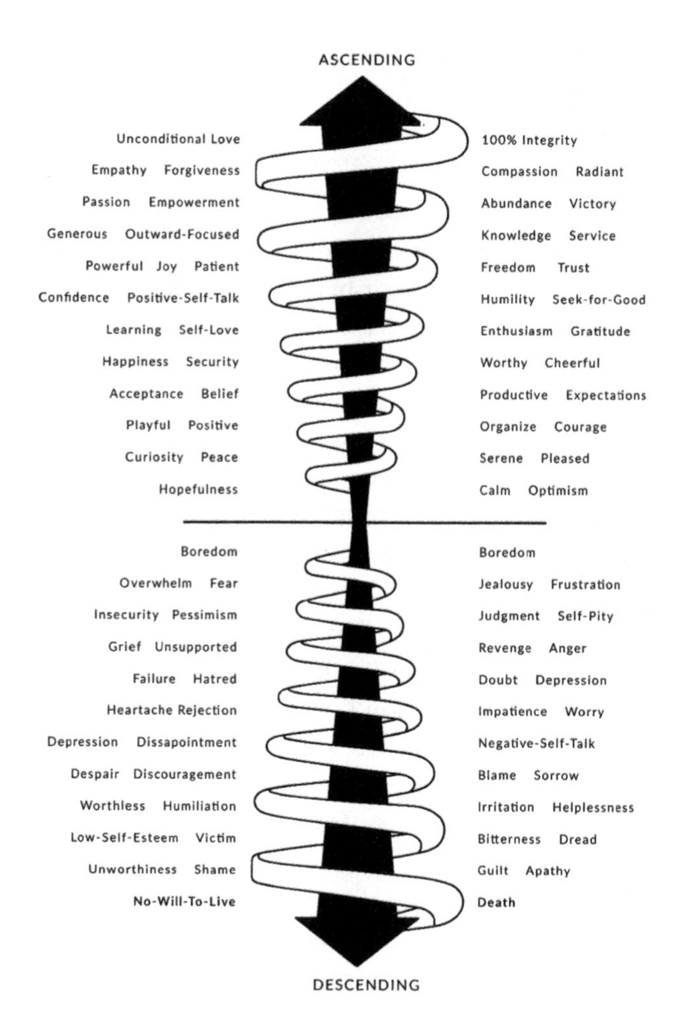

Let's quickly recap what we went over:

- There are no mistakes!
- Supposed failures are truly successes keeping you from experiencing an ordinary life.

- You have free will to make any choices you want that are neither determined by natural causality nor predestined by fate or divine will.
- Life dangles a carrot in front of you. It comes in the form of a desire you want to experience.
- The desire can be created before and tweaked after we experienced failure either directly or indirectly through outside circumstances.
- Your soul evolves through lack.
- The multidimensional lack or success mechanism is in place to cause you to consciously think and ask questions.
- It is your job to consciously monitor your thoughts, emotions, feelings, and beliefs toward satisfaction and more positive thoughts until the subconscious and unconscious minds take over the heavy lifting.
- It's the dangling of the carrot by the soul which causes you to continue to figure out what you like and don't like.

As you can see, we have more to learn as it relates to being able to *unlack* ourselves to experience more successes. Now that we know more about the lack or success mechanism, the next question is how we figure out what success actually looks like, so we know what to shoot for!

CHAPTER 7

GOOD FAILURES ASK GREAT QUESTIONS

"You're just on the other side of what you want."
—Imelda Arcilla [121]

I remember when I heard this quote from Imelda for the first time. I really gravitated toward wanting to understand it better. It was based on the universal laws that govern all existence.[122]

Think about it for a second; we live in a world where there are governing universal laws. These laws are happening to us and through us regardless of whether you know of them or even believe in them. When Imelda said this, she was referring to the Law of Polarity at the time.[123] The Law of Polarity states that everything that exists has an equal and exact opposite. For example: you cannot experience sadness without having a way to experience happiness as well.

Let's take this a step further as it relates to failure and success. You can't have a failure unless a success already exists. The failure lets you know an equal to greater success is available to you at this very moment. The only question is how do we unlock the right path to get it?

I was reading a book called, *Good Leaders Ask Great Questions* by John C. Maxwell.[124] As I was reading the book, the intuitive thought popped in my head: ***good failures ask great questions too*!**

There was another very important point that Imelda was seeking for me to address here. It had to do with how Spirit (aka your Soul) leads you on a particular path at a particular time based on your teachability index level at that moment. (This was referenced in Chapter 3.)

spirit (spir-ət/noun)

1. an animating or vital principle held to give life to physical organisms.
2. a supernatural being or essence: such as HOLY SPIRIT, SOUL sense
3. temper or disposition of mind or outlook especially when vigorous or animated in high spirits.
4. the immaterial intelligent or sentient part of a person

Marilyn Jenquin mentioned, in the same reading from the previous chapter with Imelda, of a book she read called, "Unfinished Symphonies," by Rosemary C. Brown.[125-126] This paragraph was from the inside book cover jacket I found online.

"Unfinished Symphonies is the remarkable first-person story of a widowed London housewife who is visited regularly by the spirits of Beethoven, Liszt, Chopin, Debussy, Schumann, Bach, Rachmaninov and Brahms, who talk to her and guide her hands to play and write in manuscript form music far beyond her own skills as a musician. Rosemary Brown has been investigated by experts, interviewed by Leonard Bernstein, and has been the subject of many news articles, but no one has found any indication of fraud." [127-135]

According to Marilyn, "she viewed her life with music as a failure because she had only taken a year or so of training. She felt she was not able to really do what she wanted to do because she lacked skills. Yet the composers in the Spirit World didn't see her as a failure. They viewed her as perfect for the job they had in mind, trained enough to write their music down yet not trained so much as to influence or correct what she thought it should be."

I love hearing stories like this because it forced me to ask the question, "how could Rosemary think of her life in music as a failure?" Well the answer truly lies within the perspective of both the individual and the observer.

Rosemary, in my opinion, was really being hard on herself. We do this way too much in our everyday lives thinking we must be at a certain skill level in a very short amount of time. When in all actuality you're right where you're supposed to be at that very specific moment in time!

Rosemary was a perfect vessel at this particular point in time in her life, to be able to tap into her intuitive skills and spirit abilities. She literally was able to see and listen to these musical geniuses in her living room. She was at the right moldable point in her own abilities to be open to creating these unfinished symphonies with the guidance of her incredible team of musicians.

Imagine what you can do when you are able to tap in and harness your own innate intuitive skills and abilities? This above story about Rosemary is truly another example of how there are no mistakes in life. It's all in the eye of the beholder.

Spirit (aka your Soul) will choose the perfect time for you to get access to right information for the transformational process necessary for you to fulfill your next step in the journey when you are willing to learn and change in that particular moment.

It did that with me when I retook the RICH Playbook course after Imelda's passing and ultimately in my opinion spirit is doing the same thing to you right now with you reading this book.[136] You are always able to choose with your own free will what you desire to experience next.

Just know underneath it all your soul will also continue to seek to keep you on track and it will use lack (aka the state of being without) to expose you to failure. Upon experiencing the failure your conscious mind will seek to begin to ask more questions.

Our ability to unlock success is in direct proportion to the questions we are asking regarding the failure we experienced. Only when we dig deeper, do we uncover the gems, and the path to success is revealed. This is why you should get a smile on your face when a failure arises. It truly allows you to tap into the magic that is already available for you to experience.

"Every problem is a question trying to be asked.
Every question is an answer seeking to be revealed."
—Michael Bernard Beckwith [137]

Yes, you read that right. You should get really excited when you have a massive failure because that means there is a massive success immediately waiting for you to experience. Now, all you have to do is ask the right questions to unlock the right path to obtain the massive success.

I heard this about Thomas Edison on how he worked through figuring out the invention of the light bulb, he said, "I have not failed 10,000 times. I have not failed once. I have succeeded in proving that those 10,000 ways will not work. When I have eliminated the ways that will not work, I will find the way that will work." [138-139]

He must have been asking some deep profound questions at the end of the process to unlock the answers. This method of asking questions does make a lot of common sense as well. There are many levels of questions.

Consider these two questions:

- What do I have to do to make a lot of money?
- Or, what can I create to make a lot of money?

Which question better unlocks the path to the answer? The second does, and it is what all the good failures do.

Remember Warren and Charlie – they choose to be proactive with their questions instead of reactive. They call the process Inversion.

"The way that inversion works is you take what you want to achieve, and you imagine the opposite." Productivity expert James Clear called a Warren Buffett-approved mental strategy called inversion, a "lens for looking at the world." [140-141]

Essentially, you're asking yourself: What ridiculous things should I avoid doing in order to achieve my goals?

It's the same mental model Buffett and his longtime business partner Charlie Munger used to build Berkshire Hathaway into a powerhouse. [142-144]

"It is remarkable how much long-term advantage people like us have gotten by trying to be consistently not stupid, instead of trying to be very intelligent," Munger once said in a CNBC interview.

Essentially, they look for ways not to achieve their end goal and in turn, they figure out the very actions they should avoid. Never has inversion been more prominent in their mental strategy than pages 22-23 of their Berkshire Hathaway 2010 annual report.[145] Warren said the following:

"On the facing page you can read a letter sent in 1939 by Ernest to his youngest son, my Uncle Fred. Similar letters went to his other four children. I still have the letter sent to my Aunt Alice, which I found – along with $1,000 of cash – when, as executor of her estate, I opened her safe deposit box in 1970.

Ernest never went to business school – he never in fact finished high school – but he understood the importance of liquidity as a condition for assured survival. At Berkshire, we have taken his $1,000 solution a bit further and have pledged that we will hold at least $10 billion of cash, excluding that held at our regulated utility and railroad businesses. Because of that commitment, we customarily keep at least $20 billion on hand so that we can both withstand unprecedented insurance losses (our largest to date having been about $3 billion from Katrina, the insurance industry's most expensive catastrophe) and quickly seize acquisition or investment opportunities, even during times of financial turmoil."

Earnest would keep $1,000 on hand in cash reserves that was available at a moment's notice to be used as needed. It gave him peace of mind and allowed him to navigate rough times. The letter was him letting his Alice know she too had $1,000 in reserve for the moments in time when she needed it.

In other words, $1,000 in 1939 is equivalent in purchasing power to about $18,609.93 in 2020, a difference of $17,609.93 over 81 years.[146] Now we can all learn from Ernest with a goal to have at least this much of cash on hand for an emergency.

It is the inversion mental strategy that allows Warren and Charlie to be billions of steps ahead of the rest because they ask great questions in a proactive way. Like I mentioned earlier, it takes the lack or success mechanism to wake you up to the possibility of a new experience, and you must begin to ask great questions when you're on the reactive end of failure. If you're smart, you will begin to ask great proactive questions to reap the successes more often like Warren and Charlie.

I feel after years of searching, the best way to do this is with Chris Duncan's Six Unpacking Questions to help uncover the underlying belief structure. [147]

This process of questions really works on multiple levels and should be adopted immediately going forward in both personal and business scenarios.

1. What would you like?
2. What will having that do for you?
3. What's it like right now?
4. What's your experience (emotionally) when you think about that?
5. What would someone have to believe to have that experience?
6. What else would someone have to believe to have that experience?

These questions specifically allow you to uncover the emotional charge and pain (lack) behind a particular success one wants to experience, while unpacking a core identity belief that needs to be uncovered. The emotion must be correctly aligned with the belief to successfully move forward towards a true choice (result) or desired success.

If the emotion behind the belief is not aligned with the true choice or desired success, you can see by the below image how your actions and results will quickly reinforce the belief regardless of your alignment to the belief.

BELIEF CYCLE

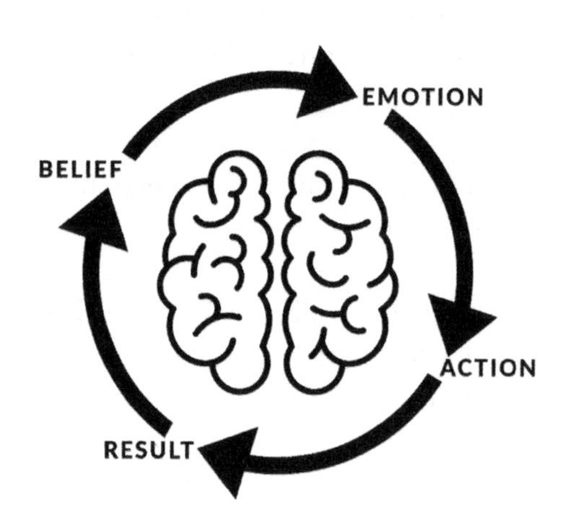

Many times our unwanted beliefs are running in our unconscious minds without our conscious knowledge of them. These questions are unbelievably effective in shortening our ability to consciously become competent of what lack or unwanted belief is running unconsciously within our mind. Our emotions and beliefs trigger our internal state of being which dictate our behaviors being expressed.

When failure comes into your current reality, it will force you to stop and ask the question as to why. Notice how this questioning instantly should be utilized to help you get a better handle on what you truly want to experience going forward without falling into the problem structure trap that was discussed earlier (in chapter 3 by Robert Fritz).[148]

Once you make a decision based on both an emotional and conscious level, it gives you confidence that you made the right, true choice. This mental strategy of asking great questions allowed me to find the right next step to take on the path to success. Now I want you to do the same thing.

Let's do a quick recap so you can consciously be competent with this information.

- Good failures ask great questions. Begin doing it much more often in your life because you're on the other side of what you want!
- Spirit (aka your Soul) leads you on a particular path at a particular time based on your teachability index level at that moment.
- Use the process of Inversion to figure out the items you should avoid doing to achieve the experience you want.
- If you're asking the question, then the answer is already waiting for you per the law of polarity. You can't have a failure unless there is an equal or greater success already awaiting your discovery of it.
- Use the six unpacking questions to uncover the unconscious lack running within your unconscious mind and bring it forth to the conscious mind. This allows you to both consciously and emotionally come to a true choice of what you want to create going forward.
- This questioning bypasses the problem structure trap and allows you to create effective true choices.

- Remember the only requirement of a true choice is just because you would love to experience it.

Now you know what failure is, why it happens to us, why people fail to have success, how it presents itself to you, and how to *unlack* to unlock the path to success through the power of questions.

This foundational information is important, so you can begin to absorb and use the ART Technique we're about to discuss in great length in the next couple of chapters as it relates to quickly turning your failure into your success.

PART 4

How to Navigate and Turn Failure into Success

CHAPTER 8

CHOOSE TRUE SUCCESS

"A civilization is as great as its dreams, and its dreams are dreamt by artists."
—Traditional Proverb [149]

For the past couple of years, Imelda had a concept of the art of RICH Living.[150] RICH stood for Reclaim your Integrity to Create Happiness. Together, we used this teaching and methodology with our clients in both their personal and business lives.

One day I was sitting down to create the enstigate™ funding solutions program, and I needed three simple steps that would easily describe the mentality and right actions necessary for anyone to follow from start to finish to get funding.[151] As I sat with a blank sheet of paper, I kept thinking about the word, art. I went to the dictionary to see the definition. (Jedi Trick: When you have an intuitive hit like that, you must immediately act on it to allow the next step to flow to you!)

art (ärt/noun)

1. the expression or application of human creative skill and imagination, typically in a visual form such as painting or sculpture, producing works to be

appreciated primarily for their beauty or emotional power.
2. a skill at doing a specified thing, typically one acquired through practice.

The art of something is what separates the masterful from the average through practice. *It is a skill set that can be learned* which makes it available to everyone who chooses to use it.

Then all of a sudden, this acronym popped in my head of *Align, Raise, and Transform*. When that happened, everything started to make more sense about the word and its acronym ART. These three words represent the word art so well. Because to create art, you must embody all three qualities to emotionally move yourself and others.

Think about it for a second. Whenever you see a world class painting, like a Picasso, what do you think was going through his mind as he was painting a picture? [152] He must have been *aligned* with the image from his brain to his hands and trusted his eyes to translate what he was envisioning to that actual canvas.

Once he started, he must have *raised* his vibration and excitement level to transfer the emotion or intention to the actual painting. Finally, the painting must be able to *transform* both the artist and the viewer if it is to be considered a piece of art. Both artist and viewer are equally transformed through the process.

The artist transforms through the experience of painting. There is a realization and level of clarity from the action of doing it. The viewer transforms through the experience of viewing the painting because the alignment and raising of the vibration creates an energetic resonance that allows you to connect on a deeper level with the artist. You actually feel what the artist must have felt when they were creating the piece of art.

That is *the secret* behind the greatest artists, coaches, athletes, actors, marketers, salesmen, politicians, speakers, entrepreneurs, and the list goes on. They all have mastered (become a skilled practitioner) the ability to align, raise, and transform a little bit better than everyone else in that specific situation. It is better known as influence.

influence (/ˈinflo͞oəns/noun)

1. the capacity to have an effect on the character, development, or behavior of someone or something, or the effect itself.

As I kept thinking about this acronym ART, it dawned on me that this can be used by anyone, at any time, to accomplish anything. It's a universal acronym that is translatable to any language, symbol, energy, focus, belief, career, situation, subject, hobby, talent, need, want, conversation, experience . . . I think you're getting the gist.

The key to becoming an artist is you must practice and become skilled in the area you seek to master. *It is a skill set that anyone can master if they choose to.* Most people fail to understand the root cause to what they are feeling and how that is affecting their daily experiences. This is the underlying reason why most people are not living a happy life all the way around. They are not aligned with their own internal guidance system.

Very few have been able to align with the correct feelings going on in their body and psyche on a daily basis. Since they are vibrating so many mixed emotions it is hindering their ability to raise their energetic set point to the tipping point level. This is necessary to transform their daily experiences to a way of living that is rich – rich in love, joy, abundance, health, friends, relationships, experiences, epiphanies, great vacations, and really wonderful food, etc.

Here's an example: A couple years back, we were asked to help raise $1.5 million for a wellness event company. They wanted to create a music festival in conjunction with a wellness event. They had a decent management team, who all seemed very accomplished in their own right in the area of the business focus, and on paper, it all made sense.

They had met with numerous investors and seemed to be getting very close to getting the money, but for some reason, they couldn't get over the hump. The only problem was this attempt to raise the money was taking way too long, like a year and a half too long. It was clear to Imelda and me that as a group (one or multiple people) they were operating with a lack and failure vibration.

When it comes to yourself, teams, marriages, couples, friends, peers, partners, and anyone in a group setting, you can only go as far as your collective vibration. Here is another analogy. If three out of the four people are operating with an abundance mindset radio channel, and the one person is operating with a lack radio channel, then the group vibration will be diminished accordingly. [153]

Remember, change can't happen until the burning desire of the group is able to collectively change the dial from the lack radio channel!

John Gottman and his wife, psychologist Julie Gottman, researched over 40 years and over 3,000 couples to create a mathematical representation called The Gottman Method for Healthy Relationships. [154]

All the observations have been quantified and turned into a kind of Dow Jones Industrial average for marital conversations. Gottman has found that marriages fall into the danger zone for divorce when the ratio of positive to negative interactions falls below five to one. Just by watching a videotape of a couple in the first few moments of a conversation about an area of marital contention, Gottman can predict with 94 percent accuracy which couples will later divorce. [155]

This is why it is incredibly important to have the leadership of any organization vibrating on the same positive frequency because it only takes one member to limit the success of the project. This is why most partnerships (marriages, businesses, groups, clubs, friendships, etc.) go through ups and downs most of the time. When one party transmits a different vibrational energy than the other person, it hinders effective communication. This makes an energetic friction, which can distance the parties very quickly.

Have you ever tried to sell something to someone when you were absolutely desperate for money? The more you needed it, the stronger that desperation was transmitted to the other person. The other person felt it, and if they weren't themselves vibrating the same desperation frequency, they would naturally be turned off by it.

We offered to help that potential client fix the team dynamics and raise their team's energetic set point to all be on the same channel of abundance for a very affordable fee. Half the management team wanted to do it and the other half didn't. This caused them to pass on the opportunity to address the deeper root causes controlling their current experience as a group.

As far as I know, they never really raised any significant money for the project, and the management team split up to focus on other opportunities. This is another case of how lack can turn out to be a really good thing because now those individuals can be pointed to the right next step for them to take on their unique journey toward success.

Another way of stating this point is there is a well-known saying by the late Jim Rohm, "You are the average of the five people you spend the most time with." When you spend a lot of time with these people, you subconsciously and unconsciously begin to observe, think and vibrate on the same frequency. This relates to the law of averages, which states the result of any given situation is the average of all outcomes. [156-158]

This is why masterminds and management training programs (clubs, groups, power couples, businesses, and partnerships, etc.) are so effective. When you get into a highly successful one where the members are very accomplished, everyone is able to observe, think and vibrate in the same way. The group dynamics will naturally elevate everyone, causing the law of averages to increase as well. You are able to get access to wonderful knowledge that allows you to elevate quicker than you would on your own.

In masterminds, you begin in the group setting, and then all of a sudden someone will express a great idea allowing the group to help fuel that discussion. Based on the observation of your peers, that alignment to the idea begins to form and excitement level begins to rise. Everyone in the group is helping to amplify the outcome of the idea. Once every member fully connects with the same vibration, knowing, and certainty of the end result, the idea will start to transform into the right next step and so on, until it transforms into an actual physical result. (Please reference Heart Math studies in Chapter 4.) [159-160]

This is also seen when you're in a group dynamic, laughing and having fun but when a negative person comes in the room, everything changes. The energetic frequency of the group is now taking on this new negative energy, and the law of averages has been directly affected. The mood regresses from laughter and joy to merely feeling satisfactory. Depending on the mood of the negative person, it could drop the group even farther down the emotional scale to frustration.

You were experiencing a really good feeling, and now you don't feel that way, and that causes frustration. You become more agitated, and this energetic anxiety is being felt. This is why it is better to leave the room when a negative person is present so your personal energetic set point can naturally rise back up to the level it was before.

Whatever challenges you're experiencing at the moment is simply the byproduct of not being able to align, raise, and transform the current situation. Therefore, once you learn how to use ART in your life, you will be able to overcome any challenge, both personally and professionally. This is the power of the ART Technique. [161]

This is why you must up level and change your energetic set point. It's the secret sauce that everyone is missing that allows them to overcome their failures and challenges and turn them into successes. Remember, MAGIC doesn't happen on the well-traveled path. Changing of the energetic channel in your vibration will give you the best opportunity to navigate your specific journey. When you combine that with the simplicity of the ART Technique, it becomes very powerful because it can overcome *all* situations.

Success (/sək'ses/noun)

1. the accomplishment of an aim or purpose.

The ART (Align, Raise, Transform) Technique has a total of nine (9) steps. These nine steps encompass the entire process which is from a failure occurring to how to properly find your path to success.

- **Step 1: ALIGN with the Right Story**
- **Step 2: ALIGN with Your Path to Success**
- **Step 3: ALIGN before Assign**
- **Step 4: RAISE your Experience**
- **Step 5: RAISE your Awareness**
- **Step 6: RAISE your Temperature**
- **Step 7: TRANSFORM through Inspired Action**
- **Step 8: TRANSFORM and Evolve**
- **Step 9: TRANSFORM with Expansion**

THE SUCCESS JOURNEY

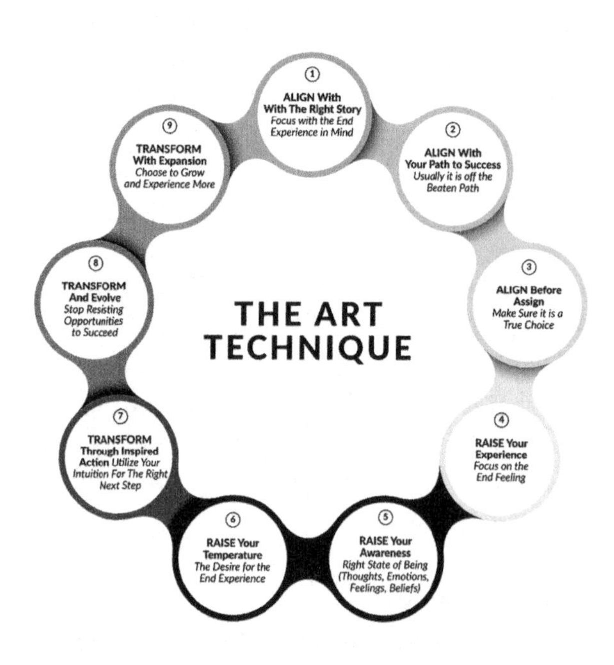

This is a guide I recommend you use until you have become unconsciously competent with all nine (9) steps. The first portion of the ART Technique is the Align section.

Step 1: ALIGN with the Right Story

Focus with the End Experience in Mind. What story are you telling yourself? I remember I was going through a rough patch as it relates to money. I was having a conversation with my dad at the time, and he said something that really caused me to contemplate my story.

"Brian you don't have to live poor anymore. I have never seen anyone live on such little money as you have! This isn't 2008 anymore. It's okay to live a rich life these days."

When Dad said this, it felt like a body punch was being delivered by Mike Tyson! [162] It hit me so hard, and it was so pure it cut through the false story I had been telling myself over the years. For days, I contemplated that statement over and over again until I began to unravel the truth for me about what story I wanted to tell myself!

I needed to align with the story I wanted to experience which meant I needed to do so first before that story could actually come into focus. I was telling the story that there are no good job opportunities out there and it is tough to make money. That was the story I was actually living for many years until I decided to change my story.

Are you living your story or someone else's? What beliefs and emotions are you currently aligned with? Our story affects our ability to handle life's circumstances. What we tell ourselves is a direct reflection on what is showing up.

This is why it is the first step in the nine-step process. You first must align with the end story you want to experience. Don't focus on the how, focus on the what. What experiences do you want to live out? (Reference chapter 7 for the six unpacking questions to help aid in this step.)

An example would be getting a standing ovation from a crowd of thousands of people chanting your name after a speech. Or it could be a simple moment of holding your newborn child in your home feeling extremely grateful. It could be a moment in time after you walked out of your boss's office, and you called your spouse to let them know you got the well-deserved promotion!

First you must focus and align with the right story! From now on, I want you to take out a notebook and/or a journal for your personal use throughout this process. You should always have a designated physical way to write down your thoughts, epiphanies, dreams, visions, inner knowing, inner voices, flashes of brilliance, etc.

I've heard that when you write down your thoughts on paper physically, it causes you to use over 10,000 different neuropathways, muscles, ligaments, etc. This instantly helps you to receive that information easier and more quickly into the subconscious and unconscious mind. You will continue to nurture this destination through your conscious mind all day. [163]

Step 2: ALIGN with Your Path to Success

Usually It Is Off the Beaten Path: Often in life the most enjoyable experiences and adventures come when we least expect it – when we ventured off the common path into a place rarely traveled.

As we discovered in a previous chapter, good failures ask great questions which will lead you to the right next step to take on your path to success. The next key to knowing if you're on the right path is to ask the question "are you off the beaten path?"

"Chances are, if you are following the crowd, you're following the wrong path."
—Bob Proctor [164]

This is where many people get caught up in the process because they are focusing their efforts in the wrong place. Who do you listen to? You must begin to observe people who have what you want and work within the structure of allowing you to come to your own decisions.

If that decision you make is leading you toward a new direction that is off course, most likely you are on the right path. The answer, the next step, will usually not come to you if this is the normal way everyone does it. It is unique to you, and it is where the answers lie awaiting your discovery.

It must be a true choice, one without a problem attached to it. One that is authentic to you. It can be anything you want to experience or create. You choose it "just because." No reasons except you'd love to have it.

This is why most programs and systems don't work for many people. First, they are telling themselves the wrong story and then they focus their efforts on a path well-traveled. If you miss the mark on both of these steps, it's easy to see why a failure is about to occur in your life because you are lacking alignment.

I'm not saying all well-traveled paths are wrong to follow. Notice the key variable and differentiator is You! If you don't believe this is the right path for you to take, then it will come true the way you believe it was going to. This path will then turn back into a failure giving you a great opportunity to return back to Step One in the process.

You will redefine what your destination will be from this new perspective. You will now align with this new path to success. Our failures are truly a gift! They are literally telling you that your internal guidance system is working and that there must be an easier and faster path available for you to experience.

Step 3: ALIGN before Assign

Make Sure It Is a True Choice: Every choice has a moment of truth. Until we properly align, we can't assign our full attention and commitment to the task at hand. This alignment is very critical and when done correctly, the successes flow to you so much easier.

Years ago, I learned this the hard way when I took a position with a start-up company. They needed a Director of Sales, and I had a track record of growing sales teams and using outside-the-box thinking. This time I was a little too far outside-the-box causing too many alignment issues going forward.

It first started with the compensation. It was not aligned for the best interests of the project. Second, the area of focus of time, as it related for their existing product and to their new product that was about to be deployed, was askew. I knew how to implement this new product in many different licensing areas; however, that was different to the vision of the leadership. Third, I was not in the same city of the company headquarters. It is very difficult to build a relationship with the people you need to be aligned with when you're not around them, especially in a start-up company.

These three (3) areas caused an alignment issue which slowly got worse and worse to the point of failure! It affected the daily decisions, the daily conversations, the daily stories being told, and ultimately, it led to a parting of ways as well.

The reason I bring this situation up is it caused some lost friendships over the years. These lost relationships have affected the alignment of mutual friends that live and work in those same circles. The leadership team and I didn't take an extra couple of weeks to get the agreement, the compensation, the future licensing opportunities, the roll out strategy, and the proper timelines aligned correctly. Most importantly, we never had a plan of attack that everyone was clear about before I accepted that job or was even offered that job.

I didn't fully understand this until I heard the phrase "Alignment before Assignment" by Mitch Huhem. [165] When you are not aligned correctly, it is very easy to miss the mark on everything you do. You will miss the mark on your health, you will miss the mark on your relationships, you will miss the mark on your mindset, you will miss the mark on your business, you will miss the mark on your focus, you will miss the mark on your sleep, you will miss the mark on everything!

Before you assign your energy, you first need to understand what that energy needs to be focused on. When you focus on the alignment, it creates the right tension structure for the successful outcome to be obtained.

The tension structure is a critical piece to the energetic resistance coming into alignment. There are two points to the tension structure. First one is what do you choose to create; which is the end destination. The second point is where are you at right now; which is the current reality you just experienced.

Both points have contrasting emotions and feelings associated with this which we will address in the raise section of the ART Technique. It is vitally important to align with the coordinates of your new destination in conjunction with where you are at right now.

Think of it as a rubber band between two fingers. One point is what you choose to create, and the other point is where you're at right now. This is the alignment piece of the tension structure. When you assign your energy to move towards your end destination this will begin to bring forth those inner beliefs and values that are in lack to the surface.

We want this to happen because it forces to surface all the doubts, beliefs, judgements and emotions that have been dormant in our unconscious minds all along. All that lack is going to begin to reveal itself to you. Write it out on a piece of paper and reveal to your conscious mind all that is holding you back from obtaining your end destination.

This allows you to meet your inner belief level about the destination. This is very important because if you set a destination that you truly believe isn't attainable, then that is exactly what is going to show up for you. It doesn't matter if you believe it in the conscious mind because it's the unconscious mind that holds the ability of change to happen.

By uncovering the inner belief level now it helps you figure out your resistance level for a change to happen. The more resistance you have to obtaining your end destination point from where you are now shows you this is an area of focus that is going to require the same level of assignment of your energy to resolve the resistance in the tension structure.

"Most people think we believe our experience. This is not true; we experience what we believe."
—Sandra Ingerman [166-167]

If you don't create the tension structure between the two points this will cause lack of tension. Lack of tension means there is no reason for you to resolve it and/or change direction to obtain your desired end destination point. No tension means no resistance; which means there is no reason for a change to occur.

Lack of tension in the align section will lead you to experience failure again and it will set you back to Step One of the process to start over. You must align before you assign your energy on a destination with the right tension structure of a true choice to give you the right coordinates going forward.

Let's recap the align section with the first three steps of the process:

1. **Align with the Right Story: Focus with the End Experience in Mind.** First step is to set your course to the right destination. Your daily story to yourself is what you're currently experiencing. Change your story, change your experience.
2. **Align with the Right Path: Usually it is Off the Beaten Path.** We are all unique individuals with very different choices and experiences. How we connect to the true experience will most likely come on a path less traveled. You will determine this path and it will resonate more as you begin to believe in it.
3. **Align Before Assign: Make Sure It Is a True Choice.** Before you assign your energy and focus, make sure you fully align with the right destination

for all the right reasons. Does the destination provide you the feeling and experience you truly want? If so, go forward with the next step in the process with a firm belief of obtaining the right end experience for you.

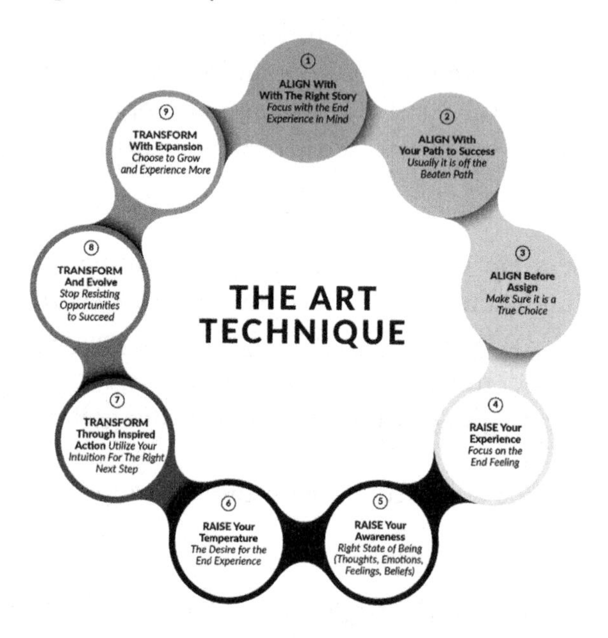

Make sure you have aligned with all three steps before you begin the Raise section. Otherwise, you will miss the mark and lack will occur sending you back to adjust your alignment in some way before you can move forward.

The second section in the ART Technique is Raise. Let's look at the next three steps on how to use that to your advantage going forward.

CHAPTER 9

REMEMBER YOUR INNATE GIFTS

"When you apply that gift you possess that comes so easily to you and can be used anywhere, anytime to help someone else; maybe your family, your community, your city, state, country or the world in general... that is your PURPOSE."

—Val Uchendu [168]

We are very powerful beings and when you remember your innate gifts, that is when everything begins to shift naturally. Everyone is being distracted by thousands of mixed messages a day through social media, television, and even through our interactions with other people.

The key is to harness your ability to consciously and unconsciously raise your experience, awareness, and temperature to the point where you effectively shift the energy in the way you want it to go per your align steps.

Now we'll go through the next three steps so you can better understand the process of how to control your thoughts, emotions, feelings, and beliefs going forward.

Step 4: RAISE Your Experience

Focus on the End Feeling. Am I doing this right? This question seems to always pop up right after you take the right next step. It's so common in the beginning of consciously understanding this process that I wanted to bring it up and give you a better explanation for it.

When you begin to raise your experience, you are solidifying the end destination of what you want to accomplish. The best way to do this is by asking yourself why do you want to experience this result? This step in the process is very important because we want to pinpoint the right feelings to associate with the destination.

You focus on raising the feelings you want to experience with the destination and allow the universe to focus on creating the directions (like on Waze) on how to get there.

A perfect analogy of this is when we use our GPS system in the car.[169] Remember my story with my mom? At no time in the process did we ever lose faith and think we would never get to the location of the game. Our only concern was how quickly we arrived.

What many people do is they know they're going the right way and somewhere in the middle of the trip they have a major traffic jam, and they start to experience long delays. The detour signs start showing that you must head back in the direction you came from.

This chain of events will usually trigger a prior experience in your past that will suddenly surface in the form of a thought, emotion, feeling, and/or belief.[170-171] This will cause you to doubt your ability to reach your destination. This doubt is there to cause you to stop and turn around to head back home to where it feels normal. Don't fall for this trick!

This is the power of the unconscious mind flexing its processing power over the conscious mind. This is why I'm bringing it up so you are consciously aware of the proverbial detour that will pop up into your experience. When this happens, rejoice and revel in the enjoyment of the wonderful gift that was given to you.

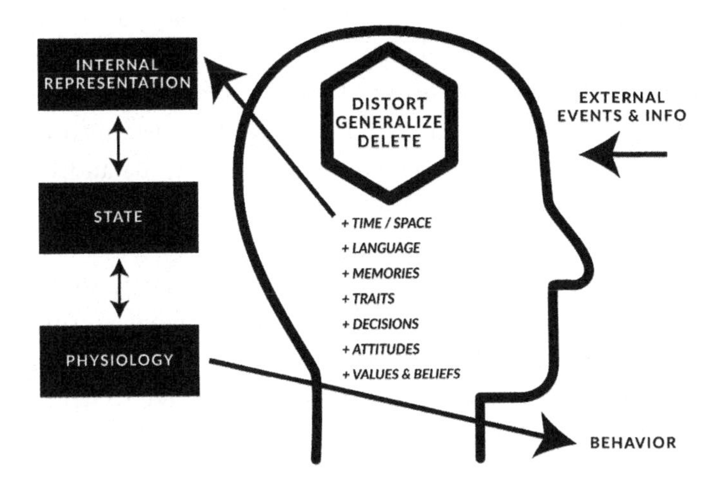

This gift is also known as an energetic set point. Have you ever begun to have some success in your life and for some reason some self-sabotaging behavior began to showcase itself at the worst possible time? Your body is so used to feeling and thinking one way that it creates an invisible set point. This doubt, this fear of the unknown requires you to reframe your thinking so as to change the habit you have become accustomed to.

The route to get there is never going to be in a straight line. It is not linear; it is not predictable. It is beyond your scope of reasoning to define it other than you don't need to know *how* you're going to get to your destination, that is *not your job.*

"Failure should be our teacher, not our undertaker. Failure is delay, not defeat. It is a temporary detour, not a dead-end. Failure is something we can avoid only by saying nothing, doing nothing, and being nothing."
—Denis Waitley [172]

You must properly set the destination of what you want to experience so the universal GPS can give you the proper directions to it. If a detour pops up, this is a great opportunity to quickly check in with your internal guidance system to see if the detour is trying to show you what needs to be addressed at this moment before the journey can continue.

Or, the detour could be showing up to help clarify that you still need to realign your end destination to what you really want to experience. Once that is done then the next right turn or road will come into focus for you to take to get back on track toward the destination!

Constantly we are second guessing and when we are trained to see the detour for what it is, it allows you to raise your confidence level accordingly. This gives us confidence in knowing that the success is coming into focus as long as we are aware of the pending detours, energetic set points, and self-sabotaging behaviors that will surface.

Once they surface, it is our job to reframe or just let go of those doubts and fears. Put them on display so you can dissipate their effect and hold on limiting you from achieving your success. Then continue back on your journey with a greater belief and inner knowing that you will actually obtain the feeling of the destination.

Step 5: RAISE your Awareness

Right State of Being (thoughts, emotions, feelings, beliefs, etc.) In a world of constant stimulation from outside forces we have lost the ability to discern our internal thoughts, feelings and emotions. Once we are able to become aware of how we are feeling, it empowers us to change the channel to a new emotion and feeling that is more satisfying to experience.

I didn't fully understand the magnitude of this step until Imelda passed away. I heard from an old manager that when someone passes away in the family or close inner circle, you can expect the productivity to drop in that person for a while during the grieving process.

He budgeted at least a month for grieving, and I feel he was way off on that assessment. It took me at least a year to come out of my shell and begin to function comfortably in my skin. Another eight months to fully remember what I wanted to experience going forward.

For the record, my productivity did improve well before the first-year mark, but I didn't feel like myself until a year after she passed. Maybe I am an extreme case, but then I came across a social experience which told me otherwise.

I joined Meetup which is an organization that allows you to create events.[173] I was in a new town, and I wanted to be social, so I joined these group events to meet new people. New Meetups get created by organizers and you get notified of them so you can go. One came through my email, and it was a new group that would bring together people who have experienced the loss of someone close to them.

It was a brand-new meetup and within the first hour, over 100 people joined. It got to the point where so many people were joining that the organizer began to send out personal questionnaires to each person making sure they were in alignment with the group's original intention. She wanted to have a place to discuss grief and best practices to come out of it better and whole again.

Many people were joining the group because they wanted to meet more people in a dating way instead of coming together in a transformational way to become whole again. This raised two immediate thoughts in my mind.

First, it told me that a lot of people are dealing with some kind of grief in their lives! If they are in the state of emotional grief, the lack channel is in full effect and they are raising more awareness to those negative emotions. That means they would attract more similar types of people who are in same radio channel frequency.

Second, this is why so many relationships end up being failed relationships. I remember one of the co-workers I was managing was always attracting the wrong type of client in her life. She was very attractive and would communicate in a very flirtatious way. This would send mix messages to the client, and they would buy the service under the wrong pretenses. When they realized that *she was not a part* of the purchase of the service, they would call the company and cancel.

She was having the same type of relationship issues in her personal life. She was attracting the same type of male persona into her life. Attractive on the outside but filled with emotional deficiencies on the inside. Remember what you are seeking is seeking you.

I tried to explain to her that this will continue to show up both personally and professionally in her life until she begins to address the emotional channel she is tuned into on a daily basis. The only way I feel I was able to come out of my grief whole so quickly was I got very in tune with my emotions.

I didn't realize how severe and costly my hidden emotions were until I came across a book called "The Emotion Code" by Dr. Bradley Nelson.[174] "The Emotion Code" is a powerful and simple way to rid yourself of unseen baggage. Releasing trapped emotions often results in the sudden disappearance of physical problems, self-sabotage, and recurring relationship difficulties.

When I came across this book, I was beginning to work in a very highly stressful sales job that was forcing me to grow beyond my usual comfort zones. Every day I would go home and release these trapped emotions that were causing me to stutter when I was nervous, to eat when I wasn't hungry, to cry when I was lonely, to self-sabotage a good situation for no reason, and the list goes on and on. This was very liberating to me because I was able to address the root emotions of lack that were leading to my many failures over the years.

Once these emotions were addressed, a weight was lifted off my shoulders and I was beginning to reveal my true authentic self again to the world. I was unlocking another major piece of the puzzle by rekindling my self-worth. Plus, I gained the confidence that I'm good at addressing my emotions because I have the tools in my proverbial tool belt to *unlack* the situation. (Now you have them as well.)

"You need to be it before you see it."

—Chris Duncan [175]

The key is you must figure out what you're feeling each day. The more you feel and stay in the emotions of satisfaction, joy, happiness, and laughter, the better. The moment you feel emotions of anxiety, sadness, depression, anger, and bitterness is when you need to take notice of them and counteract them as fast as possible.

You want to stop the momentum of unwanted emotions and thoughts before they get going. Once they get going, the momentum will attract another unwanted thought and then another. When you raise your awareness of your emotions you want to pump the brakes on the unwanted ones by trying to acknowledge what emotion you're feeling at the moment. Then assess what emotion *do* you want to get to in a logical manner.

This is where most people get screwed up. They first fail to acknowledge and dissipate the lack. (Reference chapter 6) Remember the lack is there, acting as a spotlight, to showcase what you need to focus your energy on. Don't override what you're feeling because it is there to be seen and to be made aware to your conscious mind so you can choose to change it.

Often, I come across parents, managers, business owners, and entrepreneurs who are being pulled in many different directions. You'll know it when you ask them how they're doing, and they'll state right away that they are busy.

busy (/ˈbizē/ adjective)

1. a: engaged in action
   b: being in use
2. full of activity
3. foolishly or intrusively active
4. full of distracting detail

When you are engaged in actions that are full of activities it is causing you to get distracted because you are being in use.

Have you ever tried to talk to someone who is in this state of busy?

It's very hard for them to stop and listen to what you are trying to convey to them. If it is very hard for them to stop, listen, and be present with you then how hard do you think it is for them to stop, listen, and be present with themselves?

I think you know the answer intuitively, it is almost impossible for them to stop, listen, and be present with anyone because they are unavailable. Their cognitive bandwidth is at full capacity; they lack the ability to be present. When you lack the ability to be present how can you properly address the underlying feelings eliciting the behavior of being in the state of busy?

You can't until you acknowledge the lack and dissipate the feeling behind the behavior. I remember with Imelda's passing I preferred the state of busy. I worked and worked on everyone else trying to numb the feeling of the pain and grief I was feeling inside. I didn't want to feel the lack so I did anything that would distract me fully, so I didn't have to address the underlying feelings associated with Imelda.

Only when I began to acknowledge and accept those feelings of anger, sadness, depression, and loneliness did the resistance begin to dissipate. I realized that being busy was a protection mechanism of my unconscious mind helping cope with life at that moment in time. It's impossible to create a life of happiness and joy when you're vibrating sadness and anger.

Second, it is also very difficult to just stop all together those feelings because the momentum is so strong in that direction. It's like a mile long train packed with cargo going 50 miles per hour and asking it to stop quickly. If you slam on the brakes the train will most likely jack-knife and create a huge wreck because you're asking it to do something it is unable to do at the moment.

If you ask the train operator to throttle down and apply the brakes gradually bringing the train to a halt that is a better strategy to get the end result that you want which is the train to stop and for the busy person to be in a state of inaction.

So, don't try to go from depression to happiness all in one shot. This is not realistic in any shape or form. If you try to do that, it will only fall on the deaf ears of your subconscious and unconscious mind because it doesn't want to wreck and/ or change that quickly.

Remember the unconscious mind is there to protect your quantity of life, not quality. As long as you're breathing and coping that is sufficient for the unconscious mind but for the conscious mind you want to experience the quality of life.

This means you must work within the confines of the unconscious mind to get to the end result of what you want. Which is raise your awareness to what you're feeling now and how best to change it to what you want to feel going forward.

The trick is you must gradually go from depression to anger first. Then from feeling anger to annoyance. Then from annoyance to satisfied. Then from satisfied to happy, then from happiness to blissfulness.

This process could take minutes, hours, days, months, and even years depending on the consciousness level of the person, their teachability index, their energetic set point and their inner belief of the process. I can only tell you the timeframe is different for every person, situation and end destination point.

Which is why I choose to focus on the process I have more control over and allow those timeframes to work themselves out as they need to be.

The technique I use to get my thoughts, emotions, feelings, and beliefs under my control is by meditating. This is a process you can practice, and it is crucial that you do practice it daily if you want to master success.

Below is the definition for some additional clarity.

meditate (/ˈmedəˌtāt/verb)

1. think deeply or focus one's mind for a period of time, in silence or with the aid of chanting, for religious or spiritual purposes or as a method of relaxation.

meditation (/medəˈtāSH(ə)n)/noun)

1. the action or practice of meditating.
2. a written or spoken discourse expressing considered thoughts on a subject.

I started mediating many years ago and really got into it when I wrote my first book, MeFormula: Personalized Solutions Made Easy®, in 2011. In that book, there was a section where I discussed how powerful mediation can be when utilized. I was blessed to have Imelda around because she wrote and produced a CD with both guided and unguided meditations. [176]

Imelda was trained in hypnosis and developed an ability over the years to use her intuitive connection to stimulate transformation through guided mediations. I'm so glad we went to a professional studio to get the meditations recorded in her voice. It is one of her many gifts she passed on to me and countless others over the years.

As life went on, I only meditated every Sunday when Imelda gave one of her weekly classes. When Imelda passed away, I wasn't meditating at all. As my emotions continued to sit on the depression, sadness, and anger radio channels, so were my daily experiences.

I was listening to sad songs, I was crying throughout the day, and I wasn't even leaving the house. Friends and family reached out to try to help but I tuned them out completely. No one got a return phone call and I felt I was going down a slippery slope. This was going on even after I took the RICH playbook class. My thoughts, emotions, and feelings were failing me – until I reached out to Imelda for help via Brian Dean.[177]

I was guided through an intuitive hit to reach out to Brian Dean at Caring Palms. He was a medium and was trained to connect with spirits who passed away. We held Imelda's funeral service at this location, and this was a place Imelda taught classes as well. I knew Brian would be able to communicate with Imelda and get my questions answered.

During that reading, Imelda specifically told me to promise her that I would meditate every day. The way it was articulated, if I don't do this, something bad was going to happen to me. From that day forward, every day I would take anywhere from 15-45 minutes to quiet my mind, settle my thoughts, emotions, and feelings.

Through this daily meditation, you stop all resistance and negative thoughts, emotions, and feelings. This in turn raises your emotions naturally to a more positive state of being and radio channel. Your emotions are how you change the radio station to attract the success you want to experience in your life.

If you are choosing to attract the right significant other into your life, you first must feel whole and vibrate the emotional feelings of love, happiness, laughter, and joy. You need the feelings of self-confidence, integrity, sexiness, confidence, and even feelings of desire as well.

When you feel those types of emotions represent you and you are tuned into those respective radio channels it will begin to put into motion the next step of the process to attract into your life your perfect partner, financial freedom, a new house, a great vacation, the answer to your question, or the right next step to take on your journey.

Now that you are conscious and aware of the many internal detours and solutions to those detours it will quicken your ability to find your path to success in any situation! Trust the process and reconnect with your internal thoughts, emotions, feelings, and beliefs. The failure is showing up to give you the awareness that you must first acknowledge the feeling and dissipate the resistance to it. Second you must change the channel to access the right next step to take toward successfully obtaining your destination.

Step 6: RAISE your Temperature

The Desire for the End Experience. It's getting hot in here! The key fundamental of change comes in the form of a burning desire. Only when the temperature gets to a certain degree does the water change its molecular structure (reference alchemy definition). It is no different with your desires.

"What the heart desires is medicine to it."
—Swahili Proverb [178]

I bet you never expected we would get so deep and profound? It really is one of the best tools of the universe; how it uses failure to get you involved with your life. I believe it has to do with the way we as humans are impulsed on a daily basis.

What I mean by impulse is we all have triggers that get us to do things on a daily basis. These impulse factors are used in every conversation, advertisement, human interaction, video, and the list goes on. We are impulsed everyday even if we know it or not. (Six Main Impulse Factors- FUGIJS; fear of loss, urgency, greed, indifference, positive jones effect, and power of suggestion.)[179]

The biggest proponent of using these impulse factors is our subconscious and unconscious minds as you know from the previous chapters. They have sucked up every piece of information and have created an internal operating system that gets triggered daily when you interact with life. The most powerful impulse in the human psyche by far is our inherent nature to be greedy.

We have been subtly talking about fear throughout the book, but we really need to dig into this greed impulse. Depending on your current emotion toward hearing the word greed will dictate how you feel. If you began to judge it in a negative light, then that should tell you that you have something going on with your energetic set point as it relates to greed.

When we judge something strongly (such as money, love, guns, death, terrorist, greed, politics, religion, abortion, sex, race, immigration, health care, pain, environment, power, etc.), it can cause us to attract the very thing we don't want. (Remember Gregg Braden's second mirror example in Chapter 4.)[180] This polarization of topic is an energetic trap and frankly, it causes much pain and discomfort to all who falls into its grasp.

If I said, "it's okay to be greedy," you might have immediately triggered an emotion or image of a banker on Wall Street.[181] Or you got a mental image of a specific person in your head, or you remember a time when you were greedy, and you didn't like it. This thought or memory is causing your physical and emotional state to change. This should trigger that you have some type of emotion, feeling, or point of view that needs to be reframed in some way.

Reframing your internal thoughts holds the key to unlocking your remembrance of your true authentic self. The recognition of your natural impulses is really a good thing. It means your internal GPS is working, and it is okay to have an intense desire for something when you understand and reframe it. To do that, you first need to understand the meaning and definition of the words greedy and desire.

greedy (ˈgrēdē/adjective)

1. having or showing an intense and selfish desire for something.
2. having an excessive desire.

desire (/dəˈzī(ə)r/noun)

1. a strong feeling of wanting to have something or wishing for something to happen.
2. strongly wish for or want (something).

Notice the words intense and excessive desire. These feelings translate into an energetic vibration which holds the power to transformation. Your burning desire is directly related to your ability to change the circumstances in your life. The stronger the burning desire, the faster the transformation happens through the process of alchemy.

A great example of this is when water begins to boil. Only when the temperature gets to 212°F do the water molecules begin to change shape, and a reaction occurs.[182] Up until that point, it was getting warmer, and once it crossed that threshold, an instant change happened to the molecular structure of the water. Now you can use this as your natural burning desire to change your life as well.

You can't solve a failure with the same mindset that caused the failure. Usually the success will come in a way you can't comprehend at this specific moment. Otherwise, you would have already experienced it. The universe has no filter and/or time delay on bringing you the right "next move" to take when you have a strong burning desire. This leads us back to why it is okay to have an intense and strong desire for something because that is a trigger point to change your circumstance.

Desire is natural, and it is an emotion that should be embraced more and more once you truly understand its power. The universe is abundant with infinite resources beyond your ability to comprehend. Learning how to systematically take control of your conscious, subconscious, and unconscious thoughts will lead you to a lot of successes.

Implementing some, if not all, of these simple activities into your schedule will dramatically enhance your life as well. The implications of harnessing the power of your burning desire are infinite and it will demand immediate change from the universe.

Allow the impulse to be the fuel to drive the success to you so you can have that new expanded experience. The instant the water hits 212°F, the water molecule changes form, and that works the exact same way with your thoughts, emotions, feelings, and beliefs.

I came across this gentleman named Justin Perry, an accomplished author and creator of YouAreCreators.org.[183] He heard about this affirmation technique and implemented it into his life.

For two-plus years, he completely transformed his life from being poor to becoming a millionaire all by repeating his "I Am" affirmations to himself all day every day when he had a second and in the evening. He kept saying them and listening to them while he slept at night.

"I Am" comes from Exodus 3:14. God said to Moses, "I AM WHO I AM. This is what you are to say to the Israelites: 'I AM has sent me to you'." [184] Meaning when you use an affirmation with, I Am in front of it such as, "I am happy" it is as if you are God and God is you and both are happy. If both you and God are happy, then more happy experiences will attract and show up within your life while in that state of being.

Remember, 95% of what we think every day are the same thoughts as yesterday and approximately 80% of them are negative according to the research. Justin used these affirmations each day and night to create new neuropathways in his brain in a positive way.

These new neuropathways were positive thoughts like I am rich, I am prosperous, I am abundant, I am opulent, I am a master at wealth. By doing this repeatedly, he began to retrain his subconscious and unconscious mind to accept that as his normal thoughts.

During the day in the unconscious background, his self-talk was "I am wealthy, I am substantial, I am well off, I am a prosperity magnet." He vibrated abundance and was able to tune into that radio station where the universe is able to give back to him more abundant opportunities as his burning desire increased over the course of time.

When I heard Justin's story, I immediately began to implement what he did into my daily activities. On my way to work, I would listen and say out loud the I Am affirmations in lieu of music in the car. When I went for my daily walks, I would listen to the same affirmations and say them out loud as well. While I was working on the computer, I would put the headphones on and listen to them while I worked. When I went to bed, I would put them on a loop so while I slept, I would hear them.

I have done an affirmation activity every day since, and it's been great fun implementing this. It is fun because all day, every day, I'm telling myself how amazing I am! (LOL!) This is no different than the many studies published in the "Messages of Waters" by Dr. Masaru Emoto.[185]

Emoto's conjecture evolved over the years, and his early work revolved around pseudoscientific hypotheses that water could react to positive thoughts and words and that polluted water could be cleaned through prayer and positive visualization.

Emoto said that water was a "blueprint for our reality" and that emotional "energies" and "vibrations" could change the physical structure of water. What Dr. Emoto would do is expose water in glasses to different words, pictures, or music and then freezing and examining the aesthetic properties of the resulting crystals with microscopic photography. What he found is a direct representation of why these positive affirmations work so well.

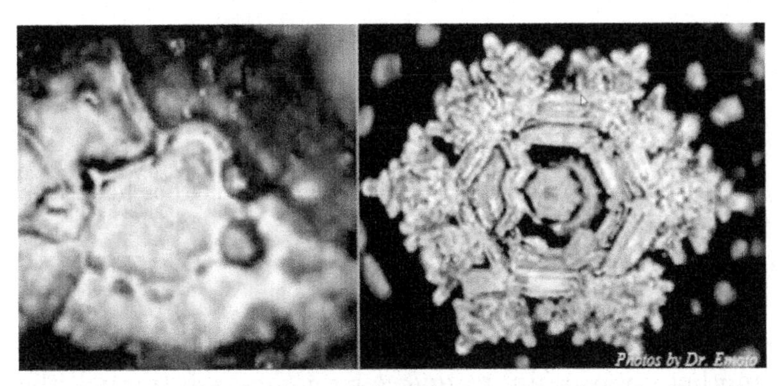

The photo on the left is of an ice crystal frozen from severly polluted water. The photo on the right is the same water refrozen after having been blessed by Dr. Emoto. One can plainly see that we do have the ability to not only heal ourselves but our Earth as well.

When the water was exposed to positive speech and thoughts it would result in a "pleasing" crystal being formed. When the water was exposed to negative speech and thoughts it would yield an "ugly" frozen crystal formation.

This is no different than how we treat ourselves on a daily basis. Think of a time when someone you love tells you how much you mean to them. You feel amazing and usually that leads to something amazing happening to you. Instead of feeling that way occasionally, I do my best to feel that way all day long!

The more positive thoughts, emotions, feelings, and beliefs I vibrate throughout the day, the better my daily experiences will be. When you add a strong burning desire in conjunction with the positive thoughts, the faster the universe and the magical process of transformation will be able to bring those experiences to you daily.

If your thoughts, emotions, feelings, and beliefs are negative and you add a burning desire, it will give you unwanted experiences on a more regular basis as well. This is why the cycle of failure will continue to show up in your life more and more.

My co-worker was attracting the wrong clients and personal relationships. Her internal guidance system was working against her. If you have negative thoughts, emotions, and beliefs toward a judgment, you will attract more people, circumstances, and situations that will reflect that back into your existence.

You will fail again and again until you recognize the lack pattern. Once you recognize the lack pattern, it allows you another opportunity to *unlack* by going back through the earlier steps in the process of success to realign with another destination to experience with this new-found perspective of consciousness.

Let's recap how to use the raise section with steps four through six of the process:

4. **Raise Your Experience: Focus on the End Feeling**. Trust the process. Allow detours to present themselves and make adjustments with your internal guidance system by keeping the tension structure in place with the end destination point.
5. **Raise Your Awareness: Right State of Being (thoughts, emotions, feelings, beliefs, etc.)** Become very conscious of your thoughts, emotions, feelings, and beliefs at all times. Become aware of the state you're feeling and acknowledge it. Dissipate the resistance and remember whatever radio channel you're tuned into will come back in return. Use meditation to begin to control your thoughts, emotions, and feelings. Retune your radio channel to what you want to experience more often.
6. **Raise Your Temperature: The Desire for the End Experience.** It's okay to have a burning desire when

you're able to reframe it and use it in a positive way. Use affirmations to raise your positive self-talk in the subconscious and unconscious mind. If you're not experiencing what you want, this burning desire will bring you failure and continue to show you a direct reflection of your negative thoughts.

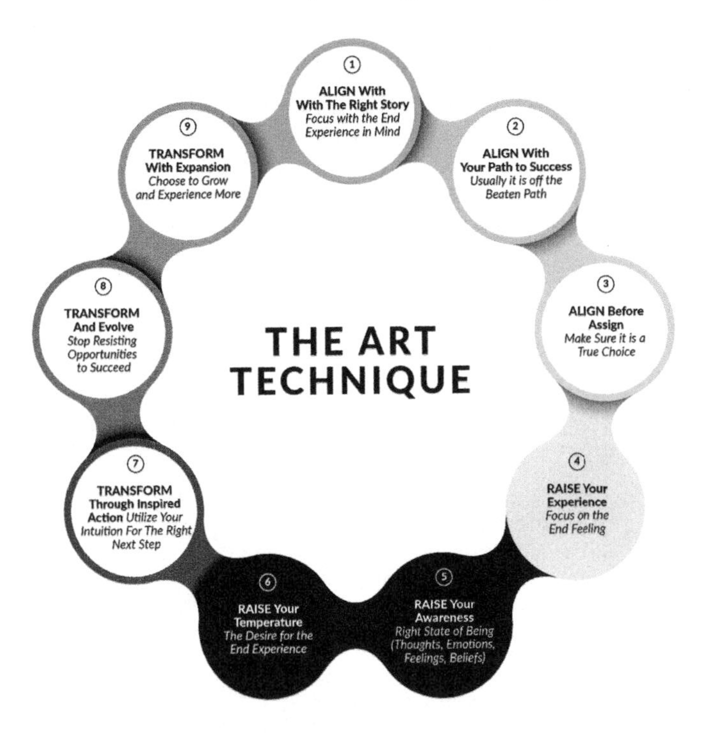

Make sure you continue to raise your thoughts, emotions, feelings, and beliefs with the aligned destination. Otherwise, you will miss the mark and a failure will occur sending you back to adjust your alignment in some way before you can move forward with the burning desire to obtain it.

Finally, let's go over the Transform Section of the ART Technique and steps seven through nine of the process.

CHAPTER 10

USE NATURE AS A GUIDE

"The most experienced 'Life Coach' you can ever imagine is Nature. She has millions of years of experience managing the entire planet."
—Bruce Lipton [186]

Life, as we know it, is all around us and has been in existence for millions of years. We are governed by universal laws that help move us, shape us, and bring forth from us transformation on many levels. The levels of consciousness are directly affected when such events take place on a moment-by-moment basis.

Every moment allows us the ability to transform through inspired action, evolving, and expansion principles like all other life forms on this planet. Use nature as a guide when it comes to connecting with your alignment and raising steps. When you do, the byproduct is the ability to transform from your current circumstance to your desired circumstance through unimaginable synchronistic and serendipitous ways.

Step 7: TRANSFORM through Inspired Action

Utilize your Intuition for the Right Next Step. Attention! Calling a friend! Often, we call a friend for their advice on what to do next. In that process, we give away our inner power and ability to pinpoint the right next step to take. Instead of calling a friend in the outer world, why not call a friend in the infinite world instead.

Why don't you begin to rely more on your inner guidance instead of relying on someone else's guidance? How is that person truly going to advise you when they don't have all the information to make a sound decision? Remember whom you should listen to.

When I say all the information, I'm taking into consideration your desires, your choices, your interests, your experiences, your intuition, your emotional connection, your natural abilities, your level of mastery of your thoughts, your beliefs, your grit, your devotion level, and the list goes on. You contain all this information. The infinite friend you should call is the *higher you (aka. superconscious, infinite intelligence, source, God, universe, etc.)*.

I was recently at a boot camp, and the presenter mentioned something that made a lot of sense to me. Suzanne Evans said, "First you need to make a decision, then you need to make the decision right!" That was a wise statement.[187]

When you make a decision, you set a new destination. Then you need to make the decision right, meaning you need to go through the rest of the "align and raise" steps until you transform through experiencing the thought, emotion, feeling, and belief you wanted to obtain in the first place.

Here is another way of looking at it. You can't have a failure without a success. The only way to obtain the success is to start the process by making a decision. Once you make a decision (a true choice), it takes mental and emotional weights off your shoulders, allowing you to focus your energy on what you truly want to experience.

It is not your job to figure out how the success is going to present itself to you. That is the job of your higher you. Your job is to focus on what and why you want to experience the fulfillment of this destination.

This allows you to feel emotionally better, releasing the resistance associated with that decision. Alleviating the resistance allows you to raise the vibration (your emotional state) and temperature to align with the experience you want.

Now you're able to go within and get an intuitive hit to act upon in a physically inspired action. To understand how to apply this to your life, let's go through the process a little bit better starting with the definition of transform.

transform (tran(t)s'fôrm/verb)

1. make a thorough or dramatic change in the form, appearance, or character of.

When something transforms, it changes and alters the appearance. This can be mental, physical, emotional, structural, spiritual, and multi-dimensional. The possibilities of transformation are endless and should be tapped into as often as you want.

Little do you know, it's happening every day of your life, with or without your knowledge. Every day you are transforming and altering your reality exponentially. When this happens without your knowledge, it defaults to your subconscious and unconscious thoughts triggering the daily transformations.

Once you start to consciously choose your end destination, you begin to embody that true choice in the subconscious mind which infiltrates the unconscious mind. It starts to transform the daily thinking, consciously and unconsciously, until they are both operating on the same system of your beliefs and desires with the same end destination.

The fastest and easiest way of doing this each day is through the power of visualization. Visualization allows the power of the ART Technique to come together through its definition.

visualization (viZH(o͞o)ələˈzāSH(ə)n/noun)

1. the representation of an object, situation, or set of information as a chart or other image.
2. formation of a mental image of something.

There have been many studies about how the brain functions when we visualize future events and feelings. I came across this particular study that focused on the neural pathway changes associated with self-affirmations and the visualization of future events in regard to their most important values.

"Self-affirmation Activates Brain Systems Associated With Self-related Processing And Reward And Is Reinforced By Future Orientation" was published in 2016 in the Social Cognitive and Affective Neuroscience.[188] The scientific research clearly stated that by utilizing visualization, we change our neuropathways along with the way we feel about the future. We physically and emotionally find it to be a rewarding experience to visualize positive future episodes.

By formatting a future mental image of something you intensely desire to feel, you will naturally allow your intuition to take over. Each of us possesses the ability to tap into our intuition at any time. It changes the way we view ourselves, and it motivates us to actually take action in the form of movement. The study showed one of the byproducts of self-affirmations and visualization of future events is how it stimulates us to become less sedentary.

You physically want to move toward the vision and the feeling you desire to experience. The more you do it, with the intensity behind it, you will illicit greater enhancement of the neuropathway within the brain. This will lead your feelings and emotions to align with your vision of the future.

I am not saying the mental image and positive self-affirmation will come true exactly the way you envision it. I am saying that this visualization technique, when done right, will give you more of the positive experiences you want in life.

When the triggers of life happen, you will be able to make better decisions and choices based on the feelings you want to experience more often. You transform any situation by how you react to it behaviorally from the feelings and emotions you want to align with.

As shown throughout our history, the outcomes are way better than what you could even imagine. The magic lies within your imagination and belief that the visualization will come to pass in divine timing.

When we were children, we naturally were able to do this all the time and get what we wanted. I was with my niece, Giuliana, the other day, and she wanted me to play school with her. She was going to be the teacher and I was going to be the student. I had just awakened and was still tired with no intention of playing school until I was fully awake.

She kept insisting we play, and she would continue to press me with the most beautiful smile and tone of voice imaginable. Her body language was strong and firm with the teacher's clip board in hand. Her intuition kicked in and she followed through without hesitation or doubt. She looked at me and said, "Do you want to draw or do math first?" Her burning desire of the feeling of fun by playing teacher with her uncle was too much for me to handle. She was influencing me naturally, and I changed my intention.

I later found out she had gone to bed the night before with this intention of playing school with me. She woke up early that morning, and was visualizing the school layout of the room, the exercises, she had the clip board, the sheets of paper, the puzzles, the crayons, etc. She was following her intuition and internal feeling of fun.

The only natural conclusion was for me to go to school that morning with her in our family room. Sure enough, the minute I said, "let's draw," I instantly felt better. I got excited about the opportunity to draw something. Her burning desire to have fun was raising my vibrations and transforming me to the point of fun as well. This is the power of visualization, intuition, and intention. I highly suggest you begin to rekindle and reconnect with yours.

I remember I had a golf outing with my brother years ago. Craig and his college friends (18+ of them) go to a new city every year and play 36 holes on Friday and 36 holes on Saturday in a Ryder Cup style format. It is fun to attend.[189] They gamble, drink, and have a blast golfing on nice courses. One year, he invited me to come. It was six months away, so I said yes, of course.

At that moment in time, I had not picked up a golf club in about two years, so I figured I had time to practice to keep from embarrassing myself. I remember saying to Imelda, "The golf outing is the best at the end because if you're one of the last groups playing, it feels like a real tournament. Everyone is watching you, cheering. Wouldn't it be great if I hit a big putt to win everyone money? That would be so much fun to experience."

Fast forward to three weeks from the golf outing. I still haven't picked up a golf club and I didn't have any time to practice because I was running my own business. I came up with a game plan that would take less than 30 minutes a day. I lived in a house that had a backyard, so every day I would go outside and swing the clubs.

I would swing the driver 20 times, then the three wood 20 times, the three iron 20 times, the four iron, five iron, six iron, seven iron, eight iron, nine iron, pitching wedge, and sand wedge 20 times. Then I would go back through the other way until I ended up with the driver at the end. Every club got 40 swings that day. So that is roughly a total of 440 swings a day. I did that for three weeks straight so approximately 9,240 swings (440 swings x 21 days = 9240 swings in total).

Let's compare this to an average round of golf of four hours if I actually went to the golf course to play. Usually, I take a practice swing or two before I hit the ball for real. As the day goes along, I begin to get tired and hit the ball without a practice swing. A normal round of golf swings/score for me is 90-110, depending on the day, plus 120+ practice swings throughout the day, for an average total of 220 swings. One day of 30-minutes of practice in the backyard (440 swings/220 swings = 2 rounds) is equivalent to two rounds of actual golf and eight hours of actual time.[190]

Take 9,240 swings divided by 220 swings for an average round that would equal 42 rounds of golf! It didn't matter if I was hitting the golf ball or not. I was building up my swing memory, so when it was time to play in the golf outing, I was mentally and physically ready. In basic terms, I was confident, and I believed I was going to play well because I had 42 rounds of golf practice in me.

Long story short, I played really well that weekend and ended up bringing our team back in the last round to win money for everyone on my team by sinking a 20+ foot putt on the 17th hole to put us ahead! It was an epic scene; 9+ grown men running around the green cheering, losing our minds. It was pure joy and happiness!

I remember driving up to the 17th green thinking, *this was the putt I was supposed to make per my conversation with Imelda six months earlier*. Everything was playing out as I visualized it. Sure enough, I was confident and nailed the putt.

Ironically, my brother was on the other team. He told me afterward, that before that putt, he feared I was going to make it. Something inside him was causing him to feel that way, so in essence we both attracted that experience to actually happen.

It was one of my best golf weekends ever, and that was only possible because I set the right destination with the right feeling I wanted to experience. I took inspired action swinging the clubs daily and visualizing the end experience I wanted as if I had already obtained it.

Daily visualization will help you get better at connecting again with your intuition. Each one of us is able to connect to our intuition at any time. Some do it better than others because they have worked on it longer. It's like working out.

The more you do it, the stronger your muscles get, and the better shape you are in. You are able to grow this skill set like you had it back when you were a child. Remember, you are already a master at this.

Visualize the feeling you want to experience for 10-15+ minutes a day as if you've already completed the destination. This is not a daydream. It's more about focusing on the result you want to experience with feelings of happiness, joy, health, excitement, satisfaction, abundance, wealth, love, desire, etc.

This is the key. You must not limit *how* the success comes into your life. The minute you say it needs to come from a specific source or person, you cut off the millions, billions, and trillions of other ways it could come to you. This means it will most likely take longer for it to come. Even if you do continue to limit the success, it will eventually come as long as you stay consistent with the belief that it will come.

This is why you focus on the destination and the feelings the experience will give you. The universe will take care of the how and where it will show up in your life. It will give you an intuitive hit which will come in any form, such as sounds, images, inner knowing, and the list is truly endless.

I get intuitive hits from headlines, social media posts, animals, books, songs, conversations, people, memories, dreams, notes, and pure gut instincts. Once you get an intuitive hit, act on it and trust it was the right next step to take. Don't judge the step. Act on it accordingly. That action will lead to another intuitive hit, and it is your job to take action on that.

As you can see, it's simple and easy to implement right away. The more consistent you are with implementing this daily visualization into your daily schedule, the better you will be in reconnecting and remembering how intuitive you really are. You were born with these abilities, and you need to use them again to speed up the process.

Once this happens, it becomes the glue that holds together the alignment and raised focus to initiate the transformation that will happen to you. In other words, it connects you with the success you have been seeking all along.

Before you can experience the transformation, you have to recognize how it usually will present itself to you in the first place. This inner feeling and knowing gives you the ability to live it now. You need to be it before you see it!

Step 8: TRANSFORM and Evolve

Stop Resisting Opportunities to Succeed. Often when success is upon us, it creates change, and in that change, a new opportunity is presented. Usually, that opportunity will show up in a form of a challenge in the very area you have been resisting for a while. Only when you say yes to it will you begin to evolve into the person you are meant to become.

Here's a real-life example on what I'm talking about. One day I was looking for a job, the one I had mentioned earlier in the book. Imelda and I were broke at the time. We needed to move the energy, so I thought there was an opportunity to get a mortgage job with the company my brother worked for.

I really didn't want to do residential mortgages again. In this case, it's a lot easier to get the loans when you work with a builder since they really incentivize the home buyers to use the in-house lender. The opportunity was in Orlando where the home buying and mortgage division was booming, which meant they needed people to support the growth.[191]

This all sounded good, so I filled out the application with my resume and cover letter. My brother used to work with one of the area managers, and that ensured I would get an interview. Everything was lining up. I would get an interview, so we moved into Imelda's parents' house for a week until an interview slot opened up.

Here is where the challenge came in. The company does their yearly budget around the time I applied, and until they got those numbers finalized, there would be no interview. This meant at least a 60-90-day delay in the perfect job acquisition plan. Now I'm in a new town (St. Petersburg, FL) and I needed to figure out a solution fast.[192]

I found three listings on Craigslist for sales manager possibilities in Orlando, when all of sudden, a unique job ad caught my eye.[193] It was a management position in Orlando, but the training would be in Tampa/St. Petersburg area. Of course, I applied, and sure enough, the next day, I get a call for an interview.

The job description was vague, so I really didn't know what the company did other than financial services. I showed up, and it turned out to be the merchant services position which I had tried years earlier without success. If I would have known it was merchant services, I would most likely have not applied in the first place.

I had a good interview. They offered a very small base—enough to cover basic expenses, but it was pretty much commission while I proved my ability to earn the management position in the Orlando area.

No one else called me, and I needed to make it happen quickly, but I still needed to get Imelda's take. Like I'd said, she was an intuitive, and I fully trusted her insight on everything, especially about this industry since I was already apprehensive. She saw a vision of me running a very successful office with a team who would be very happy working with me to achieve the goal.

I accepted the job and struggled the first two to three weeks until my talk with her in the parking lot. Ultimately, I became really good at this job and was glad to have the experience from it, which is essential to what I'm doing today with my business. Many opportunities have led to growth, and ultimately, wisdom to be used going forward.

The reason I went into a very detailed description of this story is to show how success works in our lives. The real opportunity to succeed will usually show up in the form of a challenge which will force you to grow into the person you were meant to become. In that challenge, you will come across other areas of lack which will cause you to continue to evolve and get better at deciphering what the root cause is in the situation at hand.

Most likely it's a judgement, belief, or emotion that needs to be acknowledged, reframed, and let go. If you don't address that thought, emotion, or belief, you will continue to come across more failures until you ask the right questions, which lead you to formulating the story you'll align with going forward.

When I went through this job experience, I didn't have it all figured out. The story continues because when we were in Orlando, that branch was failing. The company decided to close the branch about six months after we got there. I was given another opportunity that came in the form of a challenge: either break my lease and pay for the move to Jacksonville Beach to turn that branch around or find a new company. We moved to Jacksonville Beach, and within two months, I was able to turn that entire branch around to fulfill Imelda's vision she had when we were in the St. Petersburg area.[194]

Stop resisting the opportunities to succeed that are right in front of you. That is the quickest path to your success. It's not going to look anything like what you expect it to be. The same mind that got you into the mess most likely can't be the same mind to get you out of the mess. Only when you first make a decision can you begin the process. It's your responsibility to make that decision right by mastering the nine steps of the success process.

If you look back at your life and your defining moments, you will see how similar situations have unfolded. The people, the circumstances, and the situations might be totally different, but the method of failure will be familiar. Recognizing failure can help you properly begin the process to align, raise, and transform the situation into success.

I wanted you to continue to notice how the cycle of failure works and how the right path to success will most likely be shown to you. That should raise a question as to why failure will always continue to show up in your life, no matter what, and why you are meant to grow from it through expansion.

Step 9: TRANSFORM with Expansion

Choose to Grow and Experience More. When you expand, you begin to get in synch with how nature and the universe transforms.

"In this world you're either growing or you're dying so get in motion and grow."
—Lou Holtz [195]

When I set out on this journey to articulate my thoughts, I was challenged by multiple people, circumstances, and situations. As you learned from the previous steps, this was telling me I was on the right path because it meant I needed to grow into a better version of myself so I could fulfill my destiny. It also caused me to think about one of my all-time favorite coaches, Lou Holtz.

When I was growing up, I wasn't allowed to watch television during the week. I could watch TV for a couple of hours only on Saturday. Football is my favorite sport, and in the 80s, there was really only one team that owned college football: Notre Dame. Either you loved them or hated them. For me, when you mention Rocket Ismail, Jerome Bettis, and Tim Brown, it brings back great memories of those Saturday afternoons.[196-199]

Lou Holtz coached Notre Dame for ten seasons, took them to nine straight bowl games, and won a national championship. They competed for national championships every year, and he was the one orchestrating it. When a video of his speech came through a social media post, you bet I was all in on hearing what Coach had to say.

The speech from Coach perfectly articulated this universal law of life on growing or dying. Holtz said, "There is a rule of life that says you're either growing or you're dying. The tree's either growing or it's dying. So's grass. So's a marriage. So's your business. So's a person. Doesn't have a thing to do with age. It has everything to do with you trying to get better." [200]

When he was coaching the team and he was on top, he tried to "maintain" their program at the level it was at instead of trying to make it better. This lack of growing ultimately lead to him moving on to retirement prematurely. His regret was failing to recognize in time this universal law. You could tell this was something he thought about over the years in regard to what could have been.

This universal law has to do with a lot of situations, and I want to make a little tweak to the perception of the law. You see, everything in this world does not have to be viewed as black or white, up or down, or growing or dying, even though it is. When it comes to changing your perception and vibration on a subconscious and unconscious level, you need to become more expansive in your way of thinking.

How nature expresses the universal law is different than how most people interpret it. You need to work at growing and if not, you are actually dying. Isn't this what failure is all about? Isn't that how nature expresses the law into our lives?

The only time you are able to grow stronger muscles is when you push your muscles to the point of failure. Then your muscles breakdown and grow back stronger. The only time you are able to break through a limiting belief is when you push your desired belief to the point of failure.

There was a great experiment done in the early 1980s in the desert called the Biodome. It was an exercise to create the perfect living environment for human beings, plant, and animal life. A huge glass dome was constructed, and an artificial, controlled environment was created with purified air and water, filtered light, and so on, offering the perfect growing conditions for trees, fruits, and vegetables . . . and humans. People lived in the biodome for many months at a time, and it was wonderful because everything seemed to do well, with one exception. [201]

When the trees grew to be a certain height, they would simply topple over. It had baffled scientists for the longest time, until one day they realized the one natural element they forgot to recreate in the biodome: Wind! Trees need wind to blow against them, which in turn causes their root systems to grow deeper into the soil, which in turn supports the tree as it grows taller. [202]

This is no different in our lives as well. As we fail in a situation, we learn from it, we get mentally stronger, we get smarter, and we are able to use that experience in the future. Another word to express this meaning is wisdom. You become wiser when you are able to choose success and then another circumstance will present itself to you causing you to expand again.

"A memory without the emotional charge is called wisdom."

—Dr. Joe Dispenza [203]

This part of the lack or success mechanism is commonly referred to as "failing forward" because at the root of all failure, which is lack, is how it is in harmony with the universal push to always expand and grow. You are either growing or dying. There is no ability to simply maintain.

The other day, I watched a presentation by Bruce Lipton, and he discussed, on a cellular level, the very same concept. According to his research, cells can either be moving toward growth or moving toward protection at one particular time, thus giving us proof of the law of growing or dying on a cell level. Cells are either attracted to positive growth signals or run away and protect themselves from negative signals. [204-206]

Bruce was able to show, on a cellular level, how our bodies react to negative and positive thoughts, emotions, feelings, and beliefs. Our natural instinct allows us to move toward growth in a positive way.

If we don't feel positive, our cells literally start to shut down the ability to grow, which, in effect, shuts off our immune system and conscious ability of thought.

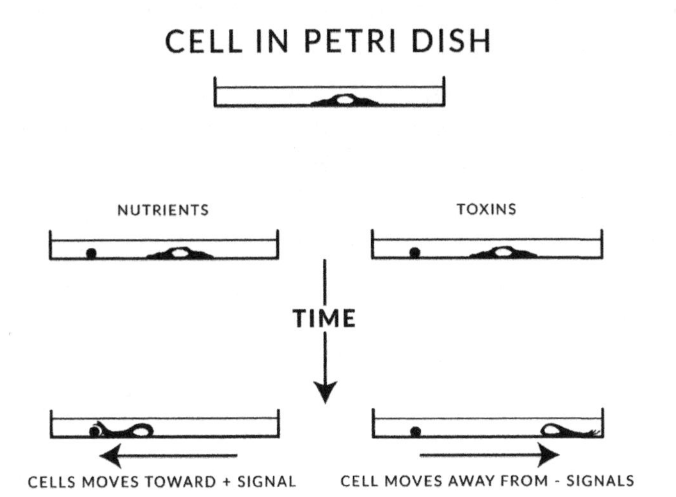

This is what stress does to our minds, body, and soul. It literally shuts down your ability to grow. When you finally push yourself to the limit, either your subconscious and unconscious mind, which is in charge of your quantity of life, will self-sabotage you to fail in some way to get your attention.

It will be small failures at first, like losing money or time; then it will lead to diseases, then ultimately, the death of someone you love will get your attention, making you ask questions and become teachable again.

Our failures are essential to our growth and up-leveling. As you become more and you're learning more, you must continue to push yourself to grow more knowledgeable.

For years, I only read sales and marketing books; I only attended these types of seminars, webinars, read these types of articles, blogs and watched these types of videos. Then one day, I hit the wall in my progression, and it started to affect me in other areas. (What is your current teachability index?) [207]

The lack of new information was beginning to take its toll. I was fatigued which caused me not to have the same amount of passion in what I was doing. This caused my sales to drop, and that caused me to lose money. In basic terms, I was beginning to fail in many areas. I was lacking growth!

Imelda told me to start reading and studying subject lines in other areas, things that were totally different like reading meta-physical and new age books, looking at art, studying animals, going to a play, learning about the body, studying something new about science, or researching my ancestry, etc. When I did, an amazing thing started to happen. I began to get intuitive hits on areas in my business that I could use to let this new-found information in.

Here's an exercise I do all the time when I'm stuck. When I can't write, when I can't concentrate on what I'm supposed to do at the moment, or when I'm bored out of my mind, I go to my bookshelf which is filled with all different types of books, CDs, and DVDs. I'm talking everything from UFOs to new age, to sales, marketing, fiction, to inspirational, to scientific, coaching programs, notebooks, etc.

I look, and I take my hand and trace the books, CDs and DVDs and wait to see if I feel an intuitive hit that might cause me to stop or pause. The minute that happens, I pull out the book and glance through it really quickly to see if anything catches my eye. If nothing catches my eye, I go to another book next to it and do the same thing. I usually see a line or headline or note that was marked in the book that is somehow relevant to what I'm going through in my life at that moment.

As you go through this process, you can quickly flip the script and get another perspective which shifts your way of thinking about the task at hand that is challenging you in your personal life and/or professional life. When you get really good at this, you will almost immediately do this throughout your day which allows you to quickly gain and grow a well-rounded perspective on any situation going on in the world. Remember, the goal is to become unconsciously competent when it comes to tapping into the magic all around us, and it happens automatically.

Now you know why failure and lack are important to grow both personally and professionally. The minute you receive the end experience you want (success), you will begin to desire something more expansive to experience. Then the lack or success mechanism will start back over again. You begin to notice you have another choice available that requires another inspired action to be connected to. This leads you to align, rise, and transform, again and again.

Every time a transformation happens through you, it allows you to grow, expand, and become more like the person you have always wanted to become. When you recognize this is happening, it gives you a sense of confidence. A feeling of happiness will exude from you, only to bring you more opportunities to succeed, evolve, and grow.

Let's recap how to use the Transform Section with steps seven through nine of the process:

7. **Transform through Inspired Action: Utilize your Intuition for the Right Next Step.** Call on your *higher you* to help give the inspired action through the form of intuition, people, circumstances, and situations. Use visualization to activate the right

movement and connection to the right next step to take.

8. **<u>Transform and Evolve:</u> Stop Resisting Opportunities to Succeed!** Only when you make a decision can you begin the process of moving forward. Usually, it will come in the form of a challenge, and it will force you to transform through the process into the person you always wanted to become. This is how you recognize you're on the right path to a successful experience.
9. **<u>Transform with Expansion:</u> Choose to Grow and Experience More.** Everything from the universe to the planet, and even to our cells is designed to always move toward growth. It is through the process of growth that we are forced to fail so we create a new form of expanded thought that will start the process all over again.

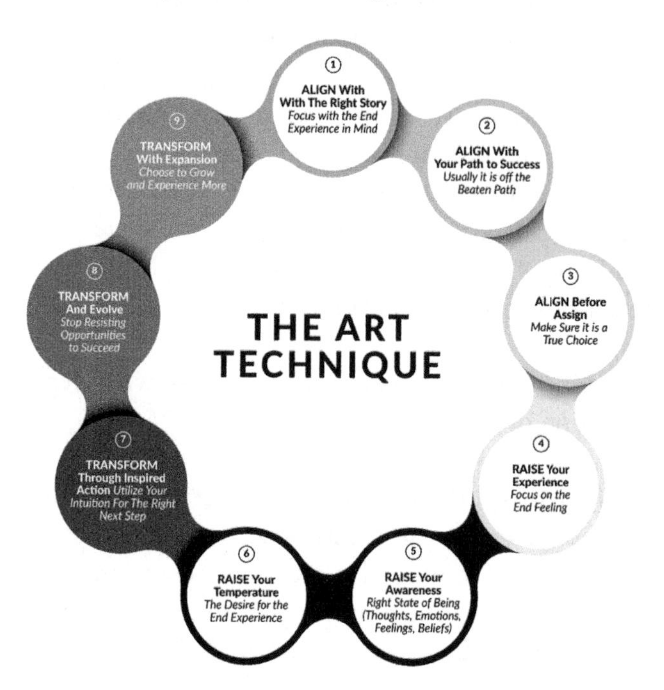

Use this nine-step process to learn how to *unlack* so you can unlock more success in your life and find a quicker path. Take a second and try to pinpoint where you are currently within these steps with your endeavors. Use this as a guide to get better acquainted with the natural flow of how you are co-creating your experiences with the environment around you.

Now you have a conscious level of understanding as it relates to the subjects of failure and success. Knowing is half the battle! You can now take the appropriate steps to manage your emotions, thoughts, feelings, beliefs, and experiences from this point forward. When you do, you will begin to tap into the MAGIC and all the benefits of life for doing so!

PART 5

Choose Mastery and How Best to Implement

CHAPTER 11

TAP INTO THE MAGIC!

"Multi-dimensional Alignment with God's Infinite Creation"
—Imelda Arcilla [208]

This above saying, acronym, and definition is what I consider the MAGIC to be. Once this is mastered, you have full control over your conscious and unconscious mind, emotions, and inner beliefs. The information you are learning becomes automatic, and you know intuitively where to direct it for a successful outcome.

This is when the magic starts in your life! It is in its truest sense the highest form of intelligence one obtains, and it is a skill one can easily master. Upon mastering it, you will be able to handle more happiness as it relates to your livelihood, abundance, health, relationships, and appearance.

Imagine no more unwarranted worries or stresses in your life. You will be able to function under pressure at a much higher level than the people around you. The overall benefits truly outweigh the skepticism of doing something you may have never tried before.

Just because you haven't knowingly tried something doesn't mean you're not good at it! Even if you have a different point of view, it doesn't mean what was written in this book was wrong either. Remember, what you seek is seeking you. If you don't believe in the magical transformational process of creation, or feel there is a better way of doing what you're currently doing, please follow your inner belief toward making that decision right!

If you are in for the long haul of choosing success, then please, let's continue to dive into tapping into the MAGIC through HUman Intelligence. I was reading a blog Imelda had written and, in the text, she mentioned the prefix "HU" in HUman. [209-212]

"We are HUmans incarnate. In Egyptian ancient culture HU meant God- Creator, so we are Godman. We have untapped abilities that are activated through these highly energetic passages that can force us to breakdown in order to have a breakthrough to our light and power." [213]

Essentially, she means when we go through a high energetic situation, either caused through planet alignments or through our experiences, we can tap into our intuition. This led me to do more research of the HU relationship to God reference, and the results piqued my curiosity further.

What caused me to remember this blog was the "HU" or otherwise known as God. We are connected to universal intelligence that is incredibly more powerful than you can ever imagine.

You, as a Godman or Godwoman, can break through the limiting situation to access that successful aim by raising your intentions (burning desire) and vibrations into alignment with the end destination. You can transform your perception and access point to obtain the transformation by receiving the right next step to take at that moment.

This dangling of the proverbial carrot and/or golden nugget will lead you to the next area on which to focus so you can move the energy and get you closer to the destination. The process continues as you begin to evolve into the person you were meant to become.

This HUman integration is already innately within you and was already provided to you before you were born. Your soul, the higher you, your superconscious and inner God connection is always on, and it's your job to connect with it often.

Years ago, I was not consciously able to connect to anything really, but now I am experiencing and interacting with this higher intelligence, and you can too.[214] The very steps laid out in this book are how I reconnected.

I don't miss a day without connecting with my inner guidance system. If there is a major decision I need to make, you better believe I don't begin the process by asking for someone else's advice. I seek the wisdom and intuition from within to point me to the right next step to take so I can receive the answer.

I humbly and graciously follow the simple nine-step process and techniques I've outlined in this book, and then I follow where my intuition leads me. If that leads me to a specific person to ask for advice, then I will receive it graciously. Then I align, raise, and transform that situation until the next failure, resistance, or intuitive hit occurs.

This is how you reconnect with your intuition and, even more importantly, remember how you reconnect with the universal intelligence. I believe this to be true, and when you do reconnect with your innate wisdom and internal guidance system, the benefits truly outweigh any risk or effort in trying this simple nine-step process to finding your path to success.

I came across a book, *Your Invisible Power,* written by Genevieve Behrend.[215] This book was short and potent with a clear explanation of how her life story evolved into becoming the only student of the leading mental science expert of her time known as Thomas Troward. Troward wrote a book called, *The Edinburgh Lectures,* which contained a passage I felt clearly explains our relationship with HUman Intelligence. [216]

"To get good results, we must properly understand our relation to the great impersonal power we are using. It is intelligent, and we are intelligent, and the two intelligences must co-operate. We must not fly in the face of the Law, expecting it to do for us what it can only do through us; and we must therefore use our intelligence with the knowledge that it is acting as the instrument of a greater intelligence; and because we have this knowledge we may and should cease from all anxiety as to the final result."

Clearly between Imelda, Genevieve, and Thomas's passages, they are all alluding that we are connected to the universal mind some people call God, source, higher intelligence, superconscious, master mind, etc. The name isn't important; it is our ability to co-operate with the greater intelligence that allows us to transform our thoughts into things, experiences, feelings, successes, and tap into the magic.

Jack Boland, minister at the Unity Church in Michigan, said, "You must believe this power can perform its mighty work within us and through us now!" [217] You are connected to a higher intelligence that created life, planets, galaxies, science, inventions, currency, and is surely infinitely more powerful than trying to do it alone.

In fact, Jack, in his book, 12 Steps to a Spiritual Experience, stated something very synchronistic with Imelda. We have an outer self which is our personality (ego) and an inner self which is our individuality (soul). Jack said, "Only until the outer man sees itself as a failure with no power can it be open and willing to accept change and connect with the power of the inner self which is soul."

The lack or success mechanism is designed to show you that you are powerless if you use the power and energy of the ego (aka self-conscious) alone. In fact, the more desire you use in conjunction with the ego the more you will experience failures. Only when you accept there is a greater force within you and choose to connect with it will you tap into the MAGIC located within your soul.

Only by observing your inner connection to the soul and believing in the infinite power can you truly tap into an intelligence that can create a desire instantly. This is the ultimate benefit of choosing success because you literally will transform and be able to experience a magical life as it was originally intended.

Over the years since Imelda has passed, I really had to figure out the best way for me to reconnect with my higher intelligence. Anything and everything was in play when it came to this initiative. Everything I have laid out in this book has been personally implemented and tested in my own life on a daily basis.

Daily I did the affirmations, meditations, and I tried hypnosis, Psyche-K, and I did a lot of subconscious reprogramming work to improve my daily outlook on life each day.[218] A lot of these activities worked, and I could see progress in many areas of my life except in the financial area. I was positive I was heading in the right direction, but with that being said, I was constantly searching for more to learn until I came across Chris Duncan! [219]

Chris, founder of The Magnetic Mind Method, did a masterclass webinar and he mentioned something that changed the game for me and supercharged my ability to tap into the MAGIC much easier. It had to deal with the wizard's gate process that he learned from Colette Streicher, author of Abundance on Demand and who is a licensed psychologist. I googled the Wizard's Gate and it led me to Ann's book. [220]

Ann Belford Ulanov, author of The Wizard's Gate: Picturing Consciousness, told a story about how a woman named Nancy was dealing with a sudden terminal brain tumor that took away her ability to speak. Ann chronicled how Nancy used pictures and drawings to articulate how she was dealing with death psychologically. [221]

These photos depicted Nancy's journey of expressing both her conscious ego and unconscious self as well. Ann chronicled Nancy's paradox of breaking her original frame of the ego while creating a new frame in how to deal with this terminal brain tumor while pushing the limits of what was true for her own life.

Earlier in the book, we discussed the law of polarity. In basic terms, you can't have a failure without having equally a success already made available to you. What was a game-changer for me was the fact Chris said *you must fully accept failure equally to the desire that you fully accept success*. That blew my mind!

Only when you get to that point, you have effectively cancelled out the resistance allowing you to enter into the wizard's gate of creation. Never thought of it that way!

It really makes a lot of sense because you dissipate the resistance of both lack of success and our innate fears of what it will take to obtain the success we want. No different than Nancy coming to grips with her lack of verbal communication and death while successfully obtaining fulfilment and success through years of extended life with clarity of her purpose as well.

Once in the wizard's gate of creation, you simply choose what you want to experience and create. When making a true choice in this state of being, there is no resistance tied to the choice and the end result is when you take inspired action, you will progress towards your destination point much quicker than expected.

To the outside looking in, it will appear magical to others and that you're getting lucky. This has nothing to do with luck; it has everything to do with the energetic structure of the true choice without resistance tied to it. That is the power of getting into the wizard's gate!

I remember just smiling and thinking about my previous conversation with Mom when I was debating if I should write about the topic failure. Mom said, "Why do you need to talk about failure so much?". At that time, I didn't have a great answer to her question until now. It is clear now that only when we get to a point of acceptance and non-judgement of completely failing will we be able to experience the acceptance and non-judgement of complete success!

If you are unwilling to allow yourself to get to that point, then you will be capped on what you are able to consciously create going forward as it relates to your desires. I'm not saying you need to stay in that feeling of failure and lack for an extended period of time. You only need to get to the point that you are not afraid of failing and take a step back from associating failure to you personally.

The final thing that was a game changer for me was when Chris said, **"Success is not personal; it is structural!"**

This means that we often associate failures and our successes to our personal self-conscious ego when it really has nothing to do with it. When I heard this, it was like a huge weight had been lifted from my shoulders. For years I would ask, "How the hell did that guy or gal get ahead in life financially? I'm smarter, but they have all this money. What were they doing that I wasn't?"

They simply had a better underlying structure when it came to making and/or saving money. Nothing more, nothing less. Over the years I have heard from people in the self-help industry that money is vibrational. You have to vibrate higher and that will somehow illicit you to attract more money into your life. Months and years would go by and I would try every morning to vibrate more money only to be let down by my current reality.

I remember one of my friends questioned me about this, and I really didn't have a great answer until Chris brought this up. This is why you can be unhappy/rich, unhappy/poor, happy/rich, and happy/poor because there is another structure at play. The personal feelings of the individual can be independent to the underlying structure of providing value to other people in exchange for money. Only when I changed the underlying structure in my business did things begin to take off for me financially.

When we changed our payment options structure to better align with our client's current situation, more clients signed up. We changed our underwriting structure with how we submitted our files to lenders and funders, and our approvals went through the roof. We changed the way we run our cash flow and allocation toward our operations which allowed us to become much more liquid. We began to change the way we delivered our service to a more scalable structure which allowed us to free up more time and deliver more value to our clients.

The key was realizing that "me, myself, and I" was not THE ONLY determining factor for the success of the business. There are other influences and underlying structures at play. It is okay for me to not have to know everything and do everything. This leads me back to the ART Technique and, most importantly, mastery of the basics when it comes to structuring your life the way you want it to be. You absolutely can structure your life and business in any way you choose.

There is no one way to do anything. There are plenty of successful structures that are working, and you can choose which ones you want to implement. That is all I did when it came to my life. I kept choosing to implement something. If it worked, great, and if it didn't, that was great too. I choose to direct my energy towards something else until it showed to be a success or a failure in my life. Either way, I was tapping into the game of MAGIC in life and business.

As I tapped into the MAGIC more often, the game began to get easier and more enjoyable to play. The financial gains began to show up more, and my manifesting abilities could be directed more towards my desires as well. The speed of actually seeing them come into physical focus improved as well. I was growing more confident, and I was beginning to stack consistent, inspired actions in a row every day, which added up really fast!

"Be MAGIC. Be in Multi-dimensional Alignment with God's Infinite Creation!"
—Brian Rassi [222]

You are already doing this each and every day. The lack of success is showing you that there is an underlying structure that is out of alignment with what you want to create. The ART Technique is a simple guide to help you get back into alignment with what you truly choose to create.

When you tap into the MAGIC, you will become a conscious creator and begin to see the physical manifestation of your desire in your life. The mastery of success and failure will only be obtained and kept if you consistently create daily practices that support your end destination you are seeking to experience.

This is why we must choose more true success in our life! This is the game of MAGIC in life and business. Every thought, structure, belief, behavior, and experience is within your control.

You get to choose how masterfully you want to play the game of life and business. Your score card is the daily tally of your experiences of being more in line with what you desire or lack. Choose to master this skillset of tapping into the MAGIC more often. It's a true choice, and anyone can obtain it with practice.

Let's recap the benefits of tapping into the MAGIC:

- Find your path to success.

- Have full control over your conscious and unconscious mind, emotions, and inner beliefs.
- Handle more happiness as it relates to your livelihood, abundance, health, relationships, and appearance.
- Tap into a greater intelligence of a higher power.
- Transform into the person you have always desired to become.
- Only when you desire being a failure as equally as you desire being a success can you enter into the Wizard's Gate of Creation.
- When in the Wizard's Gate of Creation, you can make a true choice, and it will be set in motion without resistance tied to it.
- Success is not personal; it is structural. The personal feelings of the individual can be independent to the underlying structure, providing value to other people in exchange for money.
- Choose to master your ability to tap into the MAGIC more often.

It is a bold concept that one could actually master success. It is your destiny to understand it and use it to remove the lack in your life.

CHAPTER 12

HOW TO MASTER SUCCESS

"The time that leads to mastery is dependent on the intensity of our focus."
—Robert Greene [223]

Do you choose to master success? I know you do, which is why we must start with the right end destination as a society and work our way back structurally to a more personalized approach.

success (/sək'ses/noun)

1. the accomplishment of an aim or purpose.

To do that, one must first look at the best universal structures at play and begin to integrate them in a simple daily ritual that can easily be assimilated into even the busiest schedules imaginable. It first starts with the simple choice that one may choose to master success.

Once you make that decision, it really begins to be a lot easier to move towards the life you love. For years I have been researching and implementing the truly amazing cultural principles of the ancient Phoenicians into my daily experiences. [224]

For 3000+ years, the Phoenicians ruled the high seas of the Mediterranean and trading routes with all the world's major civilizations, such as the Egyptians, Romans and the Greeks. They were one of the wealthiest, influential, and most successful societies to ever exist in our history.

My aunt, Rita George, who is the creator of the Phoenician Blueprint, first got me interested when she sent me a video (reference the notes section) about a speech she gave for The World Affairs Council. They were co-sponsoring a conference on Lebanese people with the local Lebanese Itoo Society in Peoria, IL. [225-228]

They asked Rita to deliver a speech on why the Lebanese people can assimilate quickly and succeed faster than other cultures when they immigrate. Certain members of the council were professors and had studied the various cultures in Peoria, taught International Relations at Bradley University, traveled the world, and were puzzled about this subject. [229]

Rita didn't have an answer; but upon reading many books and papers, she combined the history from Sanford Holst's books with her experience and expertise and wisdom in ancient traditions, genetics, transformational processes and practices, understanding of how to re-wire the neuro circuitry of our brains and how specific patterns are passed on in our neuropathway from one generation to another to discover the truth behind their success for centuries.

I didn't realize until the research of Aunt Rita and Carl Jung's ancestral past (please reference Chapter 5) in conjunction with Sanford Holst's research how this connection between the Phoenicians and our world governments would be as relevant as it is today. [230]

We actually have the luxury to be able to observe what societal structures have worked best over our historical existence. It is our job to utilize this knowledge to choose to create an even better societal structure than before because our societal structures ultimately dictate our societal behaviors.

Sanford Holst is a historian who researched, discovered, and wrote about the seven principles of the Phoenicians in his book called, Phoenician Secrets: Exploring the Ancient Mediterranean. [231]

What he discovered through his many years of research was how there are seven principles that made this ancient society one of the most peaceful, successful, and wealthiest for over 3000+ years.

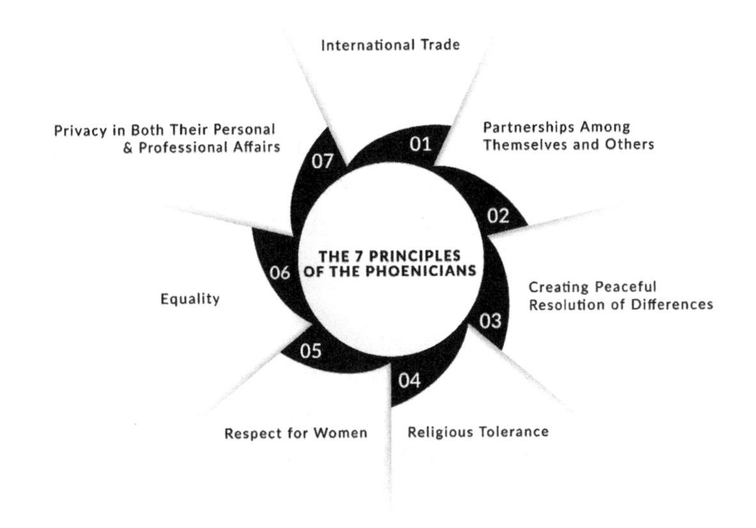

The Seven Principles of the Phoenicians:

1. International Trade
2. Partnerships Among Themselves and Others

3. Creating Peaceful Resolution of Differences
4. Religious Tolerance
5. Respect for Women
6. Equality
7. Privacy in Both Their Personal & Professional Affairs

I remember watching the video replay of my aunt, thinking to myself this would be an incredible model to facilitate in any local community, organization, and/or company structure going forward.

Remember, who should you listen to when it comes to the choice of a successful society? One that has shown the physical proof of obtaining such success for such a long extended period of time. 3000+ years (the United States of America is less than 250 years old) is a very long time, and it shows how successful this societal structure truly was. [232]

It was so successful it gives you hope that as a collective society one day in the future, enough people will be able to choose true success and get to the point of mastery within their own lives. Then, and only then, it will begin to change everything one person at a time.

Lucky for all of us, this ancestral history and ancient wisdom is already available to be tapped into by each and every individual. It can then spread to families, companies, towns, counties, states, and it even gives me goose bumps thinking it can lead to countries like the United States of America and the rest of the world!

Over the past couple of years of this entire transformation process, it has become clear to me our ancestors and our family history have a direct effect on our unconscious beliefs, and our family entanglements define our actual experiences everyday of our lives.

This in my belief is why ancestry is one of the biggest hobbies of the US, and it is our ecology (aka our relationships to one another) that we must address if we are going to be able to experience more success in our lives. It is so important to be mindful of our history because it literally is the key to our future results. [233]

ecology (/ēˈkäləjē/noun)

1. The branch of biology that deals with the relations of organisms to one another and to their physical surroundings.

Think about the struggles and beliefs your ancestors had to deal with many generations ago. Imagine if that same thought process and feelings were unconsciously running in your experience every day. That is literally happening right now within you! When I realized this, it made so much sense as to why I am the way I am. Most importantly, it defines what areas of my life I must be willing to change to be able to become what I wanted to become.

Let's talk about the logical levels of change and why they are super important as to why one person would be able to successfully change, and another would fail in the same situation.

The logical levels model was developed in the 1970s by an international expert in leadership and change management, Robert Dilts, and is based on the work of scientist and philosopher, Gregory Bateson. [234-236]

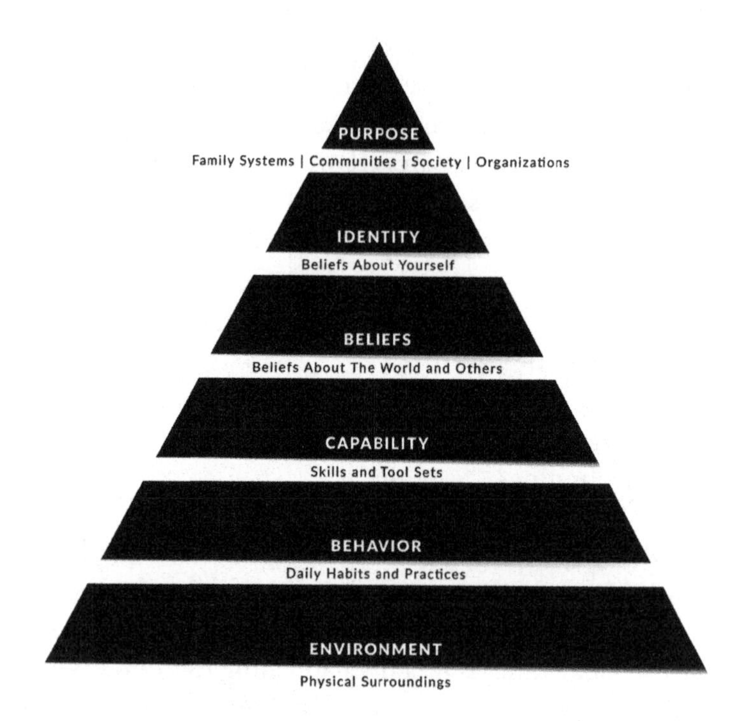

Logical Levels of Change:

1. Purpose: Family Systems (systemic) e.g., Communities/Society/Organizations
2. Identity: Beliefs About Yourself
3. Values & Beliefs: Beliefs About the World and Others
4. Capability: Skills and Tool Sets
5. Behavior: Daily Habits and Practices
6. Environment: Physical Surroundings

The key word in the Purpose level that stood out to me was systemic. Look at the definition below.

systemic (/sə'stemik/adjective)

1. Relating to a system, especially as opposed to a particular part.

This means the overall system really affects all other levels and parts of change. If you are able to address this area then you will have a profound shift in change with the people around you, not only you individually. Also, it really confirms how success is structural, which we discussed in the last chapter along with Robert Fritz's problem structure in chapter 3. [237]

I bring this up because it really is the people closest to us who directly affect our daily experience in life. This means leaders, managers, business owners, entrepreneurs, parents, teachers, and anyone in a position to influence change.

The system and the underlying structure of the family, company, management, community, society, and organization will directly affect the people within it, consciously, and more importantly, unconsciously. I want you to begin to realize the ecology and the levels of change are formed in a hierarchy fashion. This means we can affect change from the bottom up and/or from the top down. If change comes from the top down, it encompasses all the other levels of change as well!

I state this because it leads us to choose to affect change from the higher self (aka superconscious level) more than from the self-conscious (aka ego level). No different than when you affect change from the societal structure as you do within an individual structure.

There are always multiple structures at play on multi-dimensional levels as well. When you affect change on one level, it will have a ripple effect on every other structure in relationship to it. This is why major events such as our recent worldwide lockdowns in hundreds of countries regarding the Covid-19 pandemic effect change. [238]

When you effect change from the higher perspective, it directly takes into consideration all the purpose, identity, beliefs, capabilities, behaviors, and environment you are currently in. More importantly, the superconscious (aka higher self) is the best way to go about eliciting the change you're choosing because it has all the information it needs from the ancestral past all the way through to the present and even the future.

If you want to be successful more often with your true choices, seek to align, raise, and transform your current reality through the superconscious level. The superconscious level takes into consideration all the particular individual parts of the system that make you who you are currently. [239-243]

It knows how to deal with the relationships within each individual part, how to communicate with them, and most importantly reframe the conversation between them to join the teams' point of view. The team is your main personality and how you show up to the world each day.

This newfound team unity of the individual parts allows you to create change within the purpose level of change, which then creates a new, underlying structure in which all the other levels of change can take place, within and around you. Let's look at an example to better explain this point.

The simplest structure to understand would be the parent(s) / child relationship. At some point in the process, the child realizes it must do something in order to get what it wants to survive. In order to get what it wants (food, love, attention, etc.) the child quickly realizes it must follow the family structure in order to be accepted within the family.

As the child grows and begins to think consciously for itself, the friction of fitting in the ecology of the family versus becoming an adult, who is an individual expression of the family ecology, can be tumultuous. Usually once the child accepts for themselves who he/she wants to become, that friction (that resistance) will dramatically diminish between the parent(s) and the rest of family members.

You see many times the child takes on unconsciously the perceived pain and burden of the mother, father, and grandparents during their years from infancy to adolescence before they could consciously think for themselves. These beliefs are really not the beliefs of the child. They are the programmed beliefs that the child absorbed during that time frame. Many of our programmed beliefs are from our ancestral past. These beliefs will continue to run in the background unconsciously until the child grows into an adult and addresses these past, unknown beliefs which shaped their lives (thoughts, beliefs, values, emotions, etc.) all along.

This is where the connection with your superconscious (aka HUman intelligence) would be able to help. By simply asking your higher self for an acceptance of who you are and what you want to become, you can give the perceived pain and burden back to the parent(s). The infant failed to realize, however, when they took on this pain and burden they thought they were taking away the pain fully from the parent. In most cases, all they did was take on extra pain and burdens that were never meant for them to deal with in the first place.

This simple request would do wonders for that relationship between the parent(s) and the child in this case. The resistance and the internal dialogue of the child when they think about a past memory of the parent will be different going forward. The actions and intention behind the dynamics of the relationship will change for the better.

In most cases now the child has to deal with their own opportunities to grow. This helps them focus their lives on their own true choices and not try to solve the past pain and burden of the parent(s) which includes their ancestral burdens as well. That is how change can happen with the power of your very own HUman intelligence.

Another example is how outer guidance can affect your inner guidance. I use my cell phone as my alarm clock these days. It's really convenient having a tool and simple device to set up numerous alarms throughout the day. I personally use these alarms as daily reminders to wake up and to try to reconnect with my inner guidance at specific hours of the day.

This is important to me because our daily thoughts, feelings, and beliefs get reinforced through our actions which illicit our daily behaviors. Our behaviors show us what is really going on internally within us each and every day.

There was a stretch during the 2020 national lockdown and reopening of the country where I got into a phase of watching YouTube videos. I like many different types of things, and I watch many different types of videos. There was a stretch where I got caught up in the media's narrative and politics. It affected me on many different levels. [244]

The result of this binge watching of videos was the emergence of some deep, hidden, and dormant personalities that had been suppressed for a long time. What drives a particular personality is our emotions, feelings, thoughts, and beliefs. Many of our many part-time personalities which support our main personality are holding onto a belief which is being triggered by our daily interactions with the world.

In my case the political videos brought up many mixed emotions. It was like an inner tug of war going on, and it began to affect my sleep and dreams. I remember distinctly going three days in a row watching these videos into the early hours of the night and waking up with not so pleasant dreams the next day. I was tired and unable to do my full morning ritual because of it.

I'm very in tune with my inner guidance, and that intelligence transfers into my daily experience. It was clear to me I had to shut off the videos right away because I was going down a path that was in direct violation of the identity (aka values, beliefs, thoughts, feelings, etc.) I was trying to cultivate from within.

Sure enough, the next night I decided to read a new book in lieu of watching a YouTube video. I was able to go to bed on time and wake up with a rejuvenated spirit. That morning I was able to do all of my daily rituals, and the day ended up being a great success.

Our identity, our inner values and beliefs, is the key to our future successes going forward. Failures occur when we do not achieve our particular aim or specific intention. These failures start off small, and then they begin to gain momentum. Ultimately they begin to showcase themselves more and more by our actual behaviors. [245-246]

My failures started with the first political video, and then they gained momentum when I watched the second video, then the third, and so on. Soon the failures started to gain more traction when I went from one hour to two hours to three hours, etc. They continued to gain more momentum when I looked up at the clock and it was now one a.m. in the morning, and I was nowhere close to going to bed. It led to the failure to shut down my thoughts before I went to sleep, which led to the failure to have a pleasant dream state. Ultimately the failures compounded when I woke up late and I neglected to work out or do all my morning activities I like to do before I start my workday.

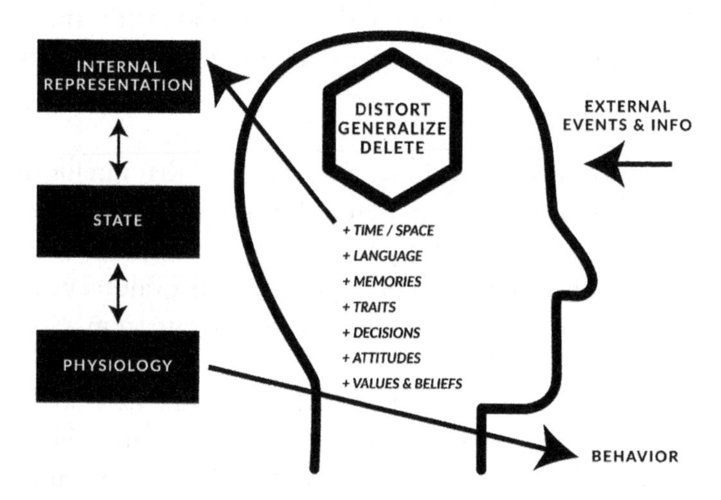

This is how our outer guidance can affect our inner guidance system thru the form of a wakeup call. When I realized my life was out of balance with my daily morning activities I was able to quickly notice them and tweak them to get back within balance with the daily structure I was choosing to experience.

These failures all started with a simple video on YouTube. It only takes one simple video, conversation, thought, ad, person, or smell to trigger a response that is in direct violation of the aim you're seeking to accomplish. If left unnoticed it can quickly gain momentum in the wrong direction. Remember, your thoughts create your reality and your experiences.

Let's define inner and outer guidance for better reference going forward.

guidance (/ˈgīdəns/noun)

1. advice or information aimed at resolving a problem or difficulty, especially as given by someone in authority.
2. the directing of the motion or position of something, especially a missile.

inner (/ˈinər/adjective)

1. situated inside or further in; internal.
2. mental or spiritual.

outer (/ˈoudər/adjective)

1. outside; external.

When I mention inner guidance, it is meant to show you that your source of information comes from within, in a spiritual or internal fashion, versus an outside source.

Inner guidance is your intuition, superconscious, beliefs, emotions, and any source of information derived from within, such as gut feelings and/or "just knowing" the information to resonate to be true.

Outer guidance is in the form of books, news, social media, people, videos, and any source of information derived from external or outside means.

In my previous example, the outside source of information was political videos from YouTube, and they blocked my internal guidance system from getting information in the form of sleep, dreams, and my morning meditations.

This is going to happen to you constantly each and every moment of the day. Our life is immersed in the perception of taking guidance in the form of outer guidance more so than inner guidance. When you're able to flip the script and immerse yourself in the form of using inner guidance in balance with your outer guidance, everything will begin to change.

We have truly been indoctrinated with an onslaught of outer guidance mechanisms that will trigger your past beliefs. When left unchecked or unnoticed by the conscious and unconscious minds, they can quickly begin to take over because the momentum is flowing in the wrong direction. It really is that sensitive of a slope when it comes to how powerfully in tune we truly are with our guidance naturally.

I remember Simon Sinek, speaker and author of Start With Why, gave an interview on Inside Quest with Tom Bilyeu called the Millennial Question, discussing the studies on how addictive cell phones, social media, and these apps have become in our daily life because they trigger a dopamine effect to the body. [247-249]

Dopamine is known as the feel-good neurotransmitter—a chemical that ferries information between neurons. The brain releases it when we eat food that we crave or while we have sex, contributing to feelings of pleasure and satisfaction as part of the reward system.

To the point he stated giving a cell phone with access to social media to a child or a teenager when used out of balance has equivalent dopamine effect as to giving them access to the ability to gamble, drink, and smoke. His point was there are age restrictions on gambling, smoking, and drinking but none on social media and/or cell phone usage.

Essentially, this dopamine effect triggers the same addictive traits during a child's and teenager's most impressionable time of development into adulthood.

This constant and never-ending stimulation of the lack going on within the child is being perpetuated in every interaction, post, video, advertisement and picture they see.

Lack of true meaningful relationships with their peers during their adolescence years will influence the thoughts, emotions, feelings, and beliefs going forward. From that point on, the child and teenager is pretty much programmed to the outer form of guidance going forward into their adult years. Remember, it's not just the child or the teenager that is affected; it's you and me as well, as shown with my YouTube video story.

This means they will be more easily controlled and influenced by outer guidance references such as media, people, leaders, marketers, and any form of misleading propaganda. When using inner guidance references such as intuitive hits and superconscious, you will be able to access more awareness to the right information to allow you to control and influence the outcome you choose to experience. That is how you master success!

We were born with all this ability to create and influence our way to experience the successful outcomes we desire. Now more than ever we must begin to harness this power; this innate HUman intelligence and use it in a way that is in direct alignment with our beliefs and values that support the identity we are choosing.

We must return to getting our information from our inner guidance and then taking it back out into the world in the form of outer guidance. In essence, you must flip the script and remember you are already masters when it comes to creating an experience that you want. If you're not experiencing the success you want in any area of your life then the physical evidence is showing you that the right next step is to begin to reconnect with your own inner guidance system.

How do you learn to reconnect and begin to trust your inner guidance system in the same way you trust your outer guidance system? Herein lies the most important point of the entire book.

You must begin to create a daily ritual that supports your inner guidance, so you can effectively use it in balance with your outer guidance. Once you do that on a consistent daily basis, you will begin to trust your innate HUman intelligence again. More importantly, allow this intelligence to work with you, and for you, in whatever area you desire going forward. This is how you master success!

After my reading with Brian Dean and Imelda (after Imelda passed away reference chapter 9), I had promised to begin to learn how to reconnect to my own innate HUman intelligence again. It started with a daily meditation for about 15-45 minutes in the morning. [250-251]

All I wanted to do was learn how to quiet my mind from the constant chatter going on from within. So, I would just set my alarm on my phone and sit in a quiet room trying to focus solely on retraining my conscious mind to slow down its thoughts.

I purposely concentrated on slowing down the momentum of the thoughts with the intent of them coming to a complete stop. Once I got them to stop, the goal was to stay there as long as I could for the rest of the time of the meditation period.

In the beginning, it felt impossible to stop the mind chatter because I had mastered the ability to stay in constant thought. I had programmed my mind to stay in constant and never-ending stimulation of thought. I lacked control and needed to regain my ability to consciously think again. The first couple of weeks were tough because it felt like I was still constantly thinking the entire time!

Then with practice, this simple exercise of quieting the mind became really easy. Within a short amount of time, I was able to master the ability to simply quiet my mind. That was a big win for me because it opened up the bandwidth of my mind to be able to receive new information instead of regurgitating old information.

This is very important. Once you open back up the bandwidth to receive new information, intuitive hits will come in! As I sat with a quiet mind for a long period of time, a random thought would pop in. It would be maybe about a person, an animal, a symbol, a color or an action, or an activity, or a feeling. Whatever it was, I took notice of it and wrote it down in my notepad next to me.

Then I would take some type of action toward that intuitive thought right after the meditation. It could be as simple as sending a text to the person that I thought of or just searching on the internet for the spiritual meaning of the color I saw.

It's important to take the inspired action toward doing what the intuitive hit has guided you to do.

Whatever feels right to you, just do it and trust that is what you needed to do at that moment. As you continue to take action toward the intuitive hits, you will begin to see more often how best to obtain the success you are seeking from them. This is how you begin to trust your own innate HUman intelligence again.

Once I mastered this piece of quieting the mind then I began to add another daily ritual in addition to the daily meditation. For me, the next step was to rekindle my ability to feel again. I would sit in a meditation state of a quite mind with the intention of feeling love. Then I would begin to notice what love felt like to me.

Where did I feel it in my body? Did it have a color to it? What thoughts or intuitive hits popped up within the meditation that I needed to take inspired action on? Slowly, I began to master my ability to feel love, then abundance, then fulfillment, then happiness, then bliss, then confidence, and many others on a more consistent conscious basis. This is how you begin to gain momentum and use your innate HUman intelligence to create more successes in your life going forward.

Then the intuitive hits began to come to me more often and not while I was in the meditative state of being. They would begin to happen throughout the day, and as they popped into my experience, I took the right next step in that moment as I thought best to do. As I took the more inspired actions and the successes began to reveal themselves more often, my trust and faith in my inner guidance began to soar.

Once I got the feelings mastered, I began to add the daily ritual of visualization with the feelings. This allowed me to begin to align, raise, and transform a true choice into my physical experience quicker because the intuitive hits were more directly related to my visualization. Once this daily ritual was mastered, I added another one (see the list at the end of this chapter).

This is how you create big changes in your life. It starts with simple daily rituals that you must implement on a consistent basis. This vision can only start with you and your life-changing devotion to MAGIC.

You have the ability to master success! It is a skill in which anyone can become fully proficient if they work at it. I'm not saying you're not going to fail ever again because that, in its very nature, defies the universal laws.

It is the unique journey, the less-traveled path that is the impetus to the greatest experiences in your life. That is why mastery is not to never experience failure again. It is to master the magical transformational process of creation in how we use the experience of failure to find the path to success!

With this book, you have a very detailed step-by-step process that gives you an excellent guide in handling failure and success but only if you practice the steps going forward. It is a wonderful compilation of information, that will dramatically shorten the learning curve, because now you know the basics and how best to use them in a structured way.

Lack leads you down the wrong direction, which leads you to experiencing circumstances in your life that you don't want, which ultimately leads you to experiencing a failure.

Failure leads you to stop and take notice to the current situation, which leads you to asking the right questions, which leads you to choose a new successful desire to experience.

When you align with this new true choice, this leads you to raise your awareness of the end result without having actually experienced it yet through the process of the daily rituals that include meditations, visualization, etc.

The process of being devoted to experiencing your true choice leads you to transforming through inspired actions which you get through tapping into your own inner guidance system (aka higher self, superconscious, God, source, etc.).

Tapping into your own inner guidance system leads you to evolve into the person you have always wanted to become through saying yes to the dangling carrot of free will which usually comes in the form of an opportunity.

As you work through the opportunity and continue to revisit the ART Technique regarding what you need to do next, you will begin to trust your own inner guidance system again which lead you to take conscious control of your own life in all areas.

As you begin to create consciously and remember you are in control of what you want to experience, this leads you to begin to trust your own innate inner wisdom which leads to tapping into the MAGIC more often.

As you tap into the MAGIC more often, it leads you to take more inspired actions toward the successful desires you choose to experience which ultimately leads you to physically experiencing more successes in your life.

As you begin to physically experience more successes in your life through this process, it leads you to trust the process more. This leads you to begin to create more purpose-driven true choices which lead you to experience more fulfillment each and every day.

When you experience more fulfillment each and every day, it leads you to be happier which leads you to living a RICH life! As you live a RICH life, it leads you to begin to affect those around you through the form of observation.

As other people see your successes through the form observing them, they will begin to take notice of what you're doing. This leads to some of them asking for guidance right away which leads to you offering them this book for the first step in their new journey.

As for the others who don't ask for guidance (those who lack direction) they will most likely continue to experience the lack from within. That lack will continue to direct them down the wrong path which will ultimately lead them to experience more failures in their lives. Then the lack or success mechanism begins all over again through the root cause of lack. Only when you *unlack* can you unlock more success in your life!

Now I want you to quickly close your eyes. Sit comfortably in a quiet place and connect with your inner HUman Intelligence. Be still, quiet the mind, breath slowly, connect, and feel the higher intelligence flowing through you right this very second. Stay in the present now moment for as long as you can. (When you're done please continue reading.)

Trust in this higher intelligence as I believe it directed you to this book. Use the tools, techniques, and documented supporting references to implement the ART Technique into your daily actions. These are simple techniques and tools you can use if you practice them on a consistent basis.

Even though they are simple to understand conceptually, it doesn't take away the daily work required to implement them. To become an artist in any profession, you must continuously practice your craft until you proficiently master it.

"Plug into the awareness of someone who has a higher-domain awareness than you do and who has already achieved the results you want to achieve, and then model exactly what they're doing."
—Mary Morrissey [252]

What the book doesn't do is provide the accountability to stay on track with your own mastery. Over the many years of dealing with people, it is usually a very specific type of individual who desires to grow and expand.

Remember when Imelda talked about devotion? (Chapter 5) "Meaning It takes consistency. It's Devotion beyond the ordinary commitment. Devotion is the superpower that sustains the rigorous challenge. It is the light in your corner that fuels your endurance to go the distance."

This type of consistency and devotion is best supported in an environment when you are accountable to the daily actions that fuel your ability to master the basics and tap into the MAGIC much more often.

This is why we want to offer you access to the Success Guide Masterclass, in addition to this book. It is a resource to aid those who choose to want more daily structure, accountability, and to fast track the learning curve with outer guidance directly related to support your own reconnection with your inner guidance. [253]

www.enstigate.com/success-guide-masterclass

It is designed to provide the support necessary to fuel those who really truly desire to master the magical transformational process of creation in a faster fashion. It allows you to shorten the learning curve by gaining the level of competency required to shift you to an inner knowing by observing and tapping into your own superconscious.

Superconscious (/ˌsoo̅pərˈkänSHəs/adjective)

1. transcending human or normal consciousness.

What makes this masterclass so magical is it involves a recode process that allows you to tap into your own higher self (aka superconscious) and let go of all the resistance holding you back from a particular end experience you desire. You can quickly change your life overnight with this process of creation in conjunction with the daily steps, accountability, and devotion. Just know this is an added resource available to those who choose to want more guidance through the process of being able to align, raise, and transform their lives consciously. To become a conscious creator!

It's one thing to know of the nine-steps; it is another thing to believe with all your existence that you are the one who is causing the failures and successes to occur in your life. You are in control of your thoughts and beliefs, which ultimately create your daily actions, which leads to your life experiences and successes.

3 ASPECTS OF CONSCIOUSNESS

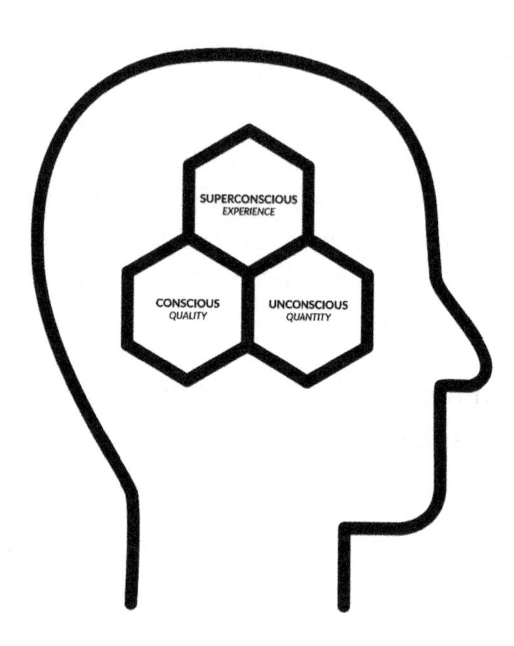

Once you've accepted this on multiple levels, without any doubt in congruence with your superconscious, unconscious and conscious mind, you have the ability to actually change your life forever! This is life-changing devotion to MAGIC. [254]

The implications of your mastery of success are so great I can't even imagine a way to quantify them. How can you quantify the positive feelings, the inner confidence, and the level of intelligence one can obtain through this success process? If a picture is worth a thousand words, the right idea could be worth millions. What is access to your infinite intelligence worth to you?

That is why I'm asking you to take this opportunity to act in accordance with your inner desire to choose to get this nine-step process mastered. The information is here to help you remember the right next step. Build your inner confidence and faith in the higher intelligence that is helping you co-create your life experience.

Will you become a master from reading this information? No! If you want to be a master, you must be a master of the basics. This book has provided that basic information on how to master success, and it is your job to choose to continue to work at it.

Practice daily the following to help rediscover your intuition and connection to your soul purpose:

- Meditate each day to tap into the intuitive hits, emotions, and feelings.
- Visualize each day to move the energy and stimulate inspired action.
- Recite positive affirmations each day to build strong neuropathways.
- Exercise, stretch, eat better, drink more water and rest more to increase your ability to feel good more often.
- Read something new every day to broaden your scope of knowledge.
- Create a daily step-by-step success guide of what you will do every day. Stay consistent and accountable.
- Sit, write, and think every day without distractions of your cell phone, tv, social media, or other people.
- Grab a notebook and write out your thoughts, intuitive hits, and things you want to create or focus on.
- Observe and get to know yourself better. Be curious and more conscious of what you do daily.

- Love yourself, smile and laugh more to create those positive emotions and feelings. Honor your journey.

If you devote yourself entirely to doing these daily actions, you will naturally find your path to success. This is exactly how I started my journey after Imelda passed away. I began to implement one daily action consistently. Then when I got the hang of it, I added another action in my daily activities, and so on.

I did not put a timetable on doing these actions. There are no deadlines when it comes to these life-changing activities. I do my best to check off as many as I can every day. If I felt I needed to do multiple meditations and visualizations, I made time for them. If I missed a day or two on a couple of items, it didn't matter because I picked it up the following day. Be consistent, be devoted, and be in a state of what you want to create. Stay focused!

As I have gone through this journey of documenting my experiences, I realized I have grown so much in such a short time span. This process of mastery and being devoted to understanding the truth of what was happening to me has allowed me to become the person I have always envisioned I would become someday.

It has shaped me in all the right areas and even stripped the pain away leaving only the wisdom to share. ***I have come to know I am here to enjoy the process of mastering my own life and to live it on my own terms the way I desire it to be.*** I only wish the same for you.

Whatever you decide going forward, be consistent, and trust the right next step is going to present itself to you at the right time. When you slow down and observe your inner thoughts, emotions, feelings, and beliefs, the universe will begin to reveal how it interacts with you.

The MAGIC is all around you now. All you need to do is remember you have these abilities already within you. Become devoted and choose true success. Remember, the MAGIC doesn't happen on the well-traveled path. You will find your path to success, and it will come when you remember you are already a Master!

APPENDICES

NOTES

Foreword

1 Duncan, Christopher M. 2019. "The Conscious Education Company, The Magnetic Mind Method, and Author of You're Not Broken." https://christophermduncan.com/.

Preface and Introduction

2 Arcilla, Imelda. 2018. "ImeldaArcilla.com." https://www.ImeldaArcilla.com/.

3 Arcilla, Imelda. 2011. "The RICH Playbook." https://www.ImeldaArcilla.com/.

4 Fairfield Resorts. 2020. "Club Wyndham Palm-Aire" https://clubwyndham.wyndhamdestinations.com/us/en/resorts/wyndham-hotels-resorts/united-states-of-america/florida/fort-lauderdale/club-wyndham-palm-aire.

5 Pompano Beach, FL. "Pompano Beach, FL." https://pompanobeachfl.gov/.

6 Wikipedia. "Indian Jones." Accessed 2019. https://en.wikipedia.org/wiki/Indiana_Jones.

7 Wikipedia. "Lara Croft: Tomb Raider." Accessed 2019. https://en.wikipedia.org/wiki/Lara_Croft:_Tomb_Raider.

8 Winfrey, Oprah. 2018. "Oprah.com" https://www.oprah.com/.

9 Wikipedia. "Richard Branson." Accessed 2019. https://en.wikipedia.org/wiki/Richard_Branson.

10 Wikipedia. "Gautama Buddha." Accessed 2019. https://en.wikipedia.org/wiki/Gautama_Buddha.

11 Dooley, Mike. 2019. *Tut.com.* https://www.tut.com/About/mikedooley.
12 KONE Corporation: 2019. "KONE." https://www.kone.com/en/.
13 San Diego, CA. 2019. "San Diego." https://www.sandiego.gov/.
14 Wells Fargo Home Mortgage. 2019. "Wells Fargo." https://www.wellsfargo.com/mortgage/.
15 Wikipedia. "Financial Crisis of 2007-2008." Accessed 2020. https://en.wikipedia.org/wiki/Financial_crisis_of_2007-2008.
16 Covey, Stephen. 2019. "Stephen Covey." https://stephencovey.com/.
17 Trudeau, Kevin. 2001. "Your Wish Is Your Command." https://www.yourwishisyourcommand.com/.
18 Wikipedia. "Shaolin Monk." Accessed 2020. https://en.wikipedia.org/wiki/Shaolin_Kung_Fu.
19 Rassi, Brian. 2018. "BrianRassi.com." https://www.brianrassi.com/.
20 Arcilla, Imelda. "MAGIC Course – Multi-Dimensional Alignment with God's Infinite Creation." Created in 2011. https://www.ImeldaArcilla.com/.

Chapter 1

21 Beckwith, Michael Bernard. 2020. "Michael Beckwith." https://michaelbeckwith.com/.
22 Mani, Anandi; Mullainathan, Sendhil; Shafir, Eldar; Zhao, Jiaying. "Poverty Impedes Cognitive Function." *Science*, August 30, 2013. http://science.sciencemag.org/content/341/6149/976.full#aff-2.
23 Holmes, Bob. "Poverty Can Sap People's Ability To Think Clearly." *NewScientist,* August 30, 2013. https://www.newscientist.com/article/dn24128-poverty-can-sap-peoples-ability-to-think-clearly/.
24 Patel, Atish: "Why Brain Power Improves After the Harvest." *Wall Street Journal*, Sept. 2, 2013.

https://blogs.wsj.com/indiarealtime/2013/09/02/why-farmers-brain-power-improves-after-the-harvest/.

25 Backman, Maurie. "Job Hopping: Why Millennials Resign Nearly Twice As Often As Older Workers." *The Motley Fool,* June 11, 2018.
https://www.usatoday.com/story/money/careers/employment-trends/2018/06/11/why-millennials-resign-more-than-older-workers/35921637/.

26 Adkins, Amy. "Millennials: The Job-Hopping Generation." *Gallup, Accessed in 2019.*
https://www.gallup.com/workplace/231587/millennials-job-hopping-generation.aspx.

27 Landrum, Sarah. "Millennials Aren't Afraid To Change Jobs, And Here's Why." *Forbes*, Nov. 10, 2017.
https://www.forbes.com/sites/sarahlandrum/2017/11/10/millennials-arent-afraid-to-change-jobs-and-heres-why/#30ef05ae19a5.

28 Nazar, Jason. "16 Surprising Statistics About Small Businesses." *Forbes*, Sept. 9, 2013.
https://www.forbes.com/sites/jasonnazar/2013/09/09/16-surprising-statistics-about-small-businesses/#6ec7774d5ec8.

29 Gerber, Michael. "The E-myth, Why Most Businesses Don't Work And What To Do About It." *Harper Business,* Oct. 14, 2004.
https://www.amazon.com/Myth-Revisited-Small-Businesses-About/dp/0887307280.

30 Arcilla, Imelda. 2011. "The RICH Playbook."
https://www.ImeldaArcilla.com/.

31 Arcilla, Imelda. "MAGIC Course – Multi-Dimensional Alignment with God's Infinite Creation." Created in 2011.
https://www.ImeldaArcilla.com/.

Chapter 2

32 Wikipedia. "Robert Baden-Powell." Accessed 2020.
https://en.wikipedia.org/wiki/Robert_Baden-Powell,_1st_Baron_Baden-Powell

33 Startup Cincy. 2020. "Startup Cincy." http://www.startupcincy.com/.

34 Tullman, Howard. "Forget About Failing Fast. If You Must, Fail Forward Instead." *Inc.*, Oct. 10, 2016. https://www.inc.com/howard-tullman/forget-about-failing-fast-if-you-must-fail-forward-instead.html.

35 Tullman, Howard. "Who Said Failure was Fashionable? Frankly, It Sucks." *Inc.*, Sept. 5, 2012. https://www.inc.com/howard-tullman/who-said-failure-was-fashionable.html.

36 Tullman, Howard. "3 Tips From Brene Brown About Failing Brilliantly." *Inc.*, Sept. 8, 2015. https://www.inc.com/howard-tullman-3-tips-from-brene-brown-about-failing-brilliantly.html.

37 Brown, Brene. 2019. "BreneBrown.com." https://www.brenebrown.com/.

38 Lester, Shane. "5 Best Books About Learning From Failure." *Medium*, Jan. 31, 2017. https://medium.com/@ShaneLester2016/5-best-books-about-learning-from-failure-db1fe8b2fac1.

39 Maxwell, John. 2019. "JohnMaxwell.com." https://www.johnmaxwell.com/.

40 Tebow, Tim. 2019. "TimTebow.com." https://timtebow.com/.

41 Godin, Seth. 2019. "SethGodin.com." https://www.sethgodin.com/.

42 Collins, Jim. 2019. "JimCollins.com." https://www.jimcollins.com/.

43 Wikipedia. "Warren Buffett." Accessed 2019. https://en.wikipedia.org/wiki/Warren_Buffett.

44 Wikipedia. "Charlie Munger." Accessed 2019. https://en.wikipedia.org/wiki/Charlie_Munger.

45 Berkshire Hathaway. 2019. "BerkshireHathaway.com." https://www.berkshirehathaway.com/.

46 Farnam Street. "The Buffett Formula: Going to Bed Smarter Than When You Woke Up." *Fs.blog*, May, 2013.

https://fs.blog/2013/05/the-buffett-formula-how-to-get-smarter/.

47 Brown, Justin. "The "Buffet Routine" Will Help You Get Smarter Every Day." 2018. https://ideapod.com/buffett-routine-will-help-get-smarter-every-day/.

48 Garmin International. 2020."Garmin.com." https://www.garmin.com/en-US/.

49 FC Cincinnati. 2019. "FCCincinnati.com." http://www.fccincinnati.com/.

50 Waze. 2019. "Waze.com." https://www.waze.com/

51 Spirit Animal Totems. 2019. "Osprey Symbolism." https://www.spirit-animals.com/osprey-symbolism/.

Chapter 3

52 Inspirational Stories. 2019. "Chinese Proverbs On Failure." https://www.inspirationalstories.com/proverbs/t/chinese-on-failure/.

53 Trudeau, Kevin. 2011. "Your Wish Is Your Command." https://www.yourwishisyourcommand.com/.

54 Ariane. "What is Teachability Index And Why This Knowledge Can Change Your Life." *Steemit*, July 19, 2017. https://steemit.com/life/@ariane/what-is-teachability-index-and-why-this-knowledge-can-change-your-life.

55 Farmer, Chris. "Professional Development Training - Teachability Index." *Corporate Coach Group*, August 4, 2015. https://corporatecoachgroup.com/blog/professional-development-training-teachability-index.

56 Green, Ph.D., Jay P; Forster, Ph.D., Greg. "The Teachability Index: Can Disadvantaged Students Learn?" *The Manhattan Institute*, September, 2004. https://www.manhattan-institute.org/pdf/ewp_06.pdf

57 Ahmed, Tolulope. "Teachability Index— How to Know How Teachable You Are." *Facebook*, October 24, 2012.

https://www.facebook.com/notes/10-laws-of-academic-excellence/teachability-indexhow-to-know-how-teachable-you-are/536049153075385.

58 Wikipedia. "Albert Einstein." Accessed on 2019. https://en.wikipedia.org/wiki/Albert_Einstein.

59 Kidd, Benjamin; Amoroso, Joseph Anthony. "The Science of Power." *Createspace Independent Publishing Platform*, November 25th, 2009. https://www.goodreads.com/book/show/9152495-the-science-of-power.

60 Hadsall, Shaun; Hadsall, Karen. 2008. "GetLeanIn12.com." https://www.getleanin12.com/.

61 Duncan, Christopher M. 2019. "The Conscious Education Company, The Magnetic Mind Method, and Author of You're Not Broken." https://christophermduncan.com/.

62 Fritz, Robert. 1989. "Robert Fritz Inc." https://www.robertfritz.com/wp/.

Chapter 4

63 Wikipedia. "Thomas J. Watson." Accessed on 2019. https://en.wikipedia.org/wiki/Thomas_J._Watson.

64 Pillay, Srinivasan. "Is There Scientific Evidence for the "Law of Attraction"?" *HuffPost*, November 17, 2011. https://www.huffpost.com/entry/is-there-scientific-evide_b_175189.

65 Kim, James K. "Scientific Proof: The Law of Attraction Is Real." *LinkedIn*, January 19, 2017. https://www.linkedin.com/pulse/scientific-proof-law-attraction-real-james-k-kim/.

66 Folger, Tim. "Does the Universe Exist if We're Not Looking?" *Discover Magazine*, v23, n6, June, 2002. http://discovermagazine.com/2002/jun/featuniverse.

67 Wikipedia. "John Archibald Wheeler." Accessed on 2019. https://en.wikipedia.org/wiki/John_Archibald_Wheeler.

68 Wikipedia. "Albert Einstein." Accessed on 2019. https://en.wikipedia.org/wiki/Albert_Einstein.

69 Wikipedia. "Niels Bohr." Accessed on 2019. https://en.wikipedia.org/wiki/Niels_Bohr.

70 Wikipedia. "Andrei Linde." Accessed on 2019. https://en.wikipedia.org/wiki/Andrei_Linde.

71 Nightingale, Earl. 2019. "EarlKightingale.com." https://earlnightingale.com/.

72 Braden, Gregg. "Missing Links – Living In A Reflected Reality." *Gaia.com*, S3:Ep4, February 7, 2019. https://www.gaia.com/video/living-reflected-reality.

73 George, Rita. 2018. "RitaGeorge.com." http://ritageorge.com/.

74 Heart Math Institute. 2019. "HeartMath.com" https://www.heartmath.com/.

75 Global Union Scientists For Peace. "Defusing World-Crises Selected References." *Gusp.org*, Accessed on 2019. https://www.gusp.org/defusing-world-crises/selected-references/.

Chapter 5

76 Arcilla, Imelda. 2018. "ImeldaArcilla.com." https://www.ImeldaArcilla.com/.

77 Wikipedia. "National Football League." Accessed in 2019. https://en.wikipedia.org/wiki/National_Football_League.

78 Pivotal Education. "Levels of Competence." Accessed on 2019. https://pivotaleducation.com/hidden-trainer-area/training-online-resources/levels-of-competence/.

79 Wikipedia. "Four Stages of Competence." Accessed on 2019. https://en.wikipedia.org/wiki/Four_stages_of_competence.

80 Trudeau, Kevin. 2011. "Your Wish Is Your Command." https://www.yourwishisyourcommand.com/.

81 Winget, Larry. 2019. "Larry Winget: The Pitbull of Personal Development®." https://www.larrywinget.com/.

82 Perrin, Andrew. "Slightly fewer Americans are reading print books, new survey finds." Pew Research, Oct. 19, 2015. https://www.pewresearch.org/fact-tank/2015/10/19/slightly-fewer-americans-are-reading-print-books-new-survey-finds/.

83 Whittington, Thomas. "How Many Books Does the Average Person Read?" *Iris Reading*, October 7, 2016. https://www.irisreading.com/how-many-books-does-the-averag e-person-read/.

84 Gladwell, Malcom. "Outliners: The Story of Success." *Wikipedia*, Accessed on 2019. https://en.wikipedia.org/wiki/Outliers_(book)

85 Arcilla, Imelda. "Woman's Entrepreneurs Radio: Evolving Through Entrepreneurship." Interview by Deborah A. Bailey. *Women's Entrepreneur Radio*, May 24, 2017. https://sacredaffirmation.podbean.com/e/evolving-through-entrepreneurship/.

86 Wikipedia. "Santiago Ramón y Cajal." Accessed on 2019. https://en.wikipedia.org/wiki/Santiago_Ramon_y_Cajal.

87 The Brain From Top To Bottom. "Plasticity In Neural Networks." *The Brian*, Accessed on 2019. http://thebrain.mcgill.ca/flash/d/d_07/d_07_cl/d_07_cl_tra/d_07_cl_tra.html.

88 The Mind Unleashed. "The Conscious, Subconscious, And Unconscious Mind – How Does It All Work?" *The Mind Unleashed*, Accessed on 2019. https://themindunleashed.com/2014/03/conscious-subconscious-unconscious-mind-work.html.

89 Wikipedia. "Sigmund Freud." Accessed on 2019. https://en.wikipedia.org/wiki/Sigmund_Freud.

90 Harvard Health Publishing. "Unconscious or Subconscious?" *Harvard Health Blog*, August 2, 2010. https://www.health.harvard.edu/blog/unconscious-or-subconscious-20100801255.

91 Wikipedia. "Carl Jung." Accessed on 2019. https://en.wikipedia.org/wiki/Carl_Jung.

92 McLeod, Carl. "Carl Jung." *Simply Psychology*, Published 2008. https://www.simplypsychology.org/carl-jung.html.

93 Taylor, Justin. "Why The Law of Attraction Is So Difficult." Werdsmith, Accessed on 2021. https://werdsmith.com/genesology/5HKuVjbDc

94 Antanaityte, Neringa. "Mind Matters: How To Effortlessly Have More Positive Thoughts." *Tlex Institute*, Accessed on 2019. https://tlexinstitute.com/how-to-effortlessly-have-more-positive-thoughts/

95 Lipton, PhD., Bruce H. "The Biology of Belief." *Amazon*, October 11, 2016. https://www.amazon.com/Biology-Belief-10th-Anniversary-Consciousness/dp/140195247X/.

96 Lally, Phillippa; H. M. van Jaarsveld, Cornelia; Potts, Henry W. W.; Wardle, Jane. "How Are Habits Formed: Modelling Habit Formation In The Real World." *European Journal of Social Psychology, Wile Online Library*, July 16, 2009. https://onlinelibrary.wiley.com/doi/full/10.1002/ejsp.674

97 Wikipedia. "Bit." Accessed on 2019. https://en.wikipedia.org/wiki/Bit

98 TechTerms. "What is the difference between a 32-bit and 64-bit system?" *TechTerms*, July 19, 2017. https://techterms.com/help/difference_between_32-bit_and_64-bit_systems.

99 Corbett, Sara. "The Holy Grail of the Unconscious." *The New York Times Magazine*, Sept. 16, 2009. https://www.nytimes.com/2009/09/20/magazine/20jung-t.html.

100 Davis, Ph.D., Bruce. "There Are 50,000 Thoughts Standing Between You and Your Partner Every Day!" *HuffPost*, July 23, 2013. https://www.huffpost.com/entry/healthy-relationships_b_3307916.

101 Faith Hope & Psychology. "80 % of Thoughts Are Negative...95 % Are Repetitive." *Faith Hope & Psychology*, March 2, 2012.

https://faithhopeandpsychology.wordpress.com/2012/03/02/80-of-thoughts-are-negative-95-are-repetitive/

102 Clear, James. "How Long Does it Actually Take to Form a New Habit? (Backed by Science)" *JamesClear.com*, Accessed on 2019. https://jamesclear.com/new-habit.

Chapter 6

103 Jenquin, Marilyn. 1998. "International Foundation for Spiritual Knowledge (IFSK)." http://ifsk.org/

104 Zoom. 2021. "Zoom." https://zoom.us/.

105 Arcilla, Imelda. 2018. "ImeldaArcilla.com." https://www.ImeldaArcilla.com/.

106 George, Robert. 2021. "Robert George." https://www.imdb.com/name/nm0313593/.

107 Los Angeles, CA. 2019. "Los Angeles." https://www.lacity.org/.

108 Red Bull. 2019. "RedBull.com." https://www.redbull.com/us-en/.

109 The University of Iowa. 2019. "University of Iowa." https://uiowa.edu/.

110 Wikipedia. "Big Ten Conference." Accessed on 2019. https://en.wikipedia.org/wiki/Big_Ten_Conference

111 Jenquin, Marilyn. 1998. "International Foundation for Spiritual Knowledge (IFSK)." http://ifsk.org/

112 Wikipedia. "Carrot and Stick." Accessed on 2019. https://en.wikipedia.org/wiki/Carrot_and_stick.

113 Rassi, Brian. 2018. "BrianRassi.com" https://www.brianrassi.com/.

114 Wikipedia. "Hurricane Katrina." Accessed on 2019. https://en.wikipedia.org/wiki/Hurricane_Katrina.

115 Edwards, Chris. "Hurricane Katrina: Remembering the Federal Failures." *CATO Institute*, August 27, 2015. https://www.cato.org/blog/hurricane-katrina-remembering-federal-failures.

116 Wikipedia. "2005 Levee Failures In Greater New Orleans." Accessed on 2019.

https://en.wikipedia.org/wiki/2005_levee_failures_in_Greater_New_Orleans

117 Griffis, F.H. (Bud). "Engineering Failures Exposed By Hurricane Katrina." *ScienceDirect*, Volume 29, Issue 2, April 2007, Pages 189-195.
https://www.sciencedirect.com/science/article/pii/S0160791X07000097.

118 Wikipedia. "HAARP." Accessed on 2019.
https://en.wikipedia.org/wiki/High-frequency_Active_Auroral_Research_Program.

119 Wikipedia. "FM Broadcasting." Accessed on 2019.
https://en.wikipedia.org/wiki/FM_broadcasting.

120 Hicks, Esther and Jerry. "Ask and It Is Given: Learning to Manifest Your Desires." *Hay House Inc., Amazon*, October 1, 2004.
https://www.amazon.com/Ask-Given-Learning-Manifest-Attraction-ebook/dp/B00DJ735O4.

Chapter 7

121 Arcilla, Imelda. 2018. "ImeldaArcilla.com."
https://www.ImeldaArcilla.com/.

122 Regan, Sarah. "The 12 Universal Laws & How To Practice Them." *mbg Spirituality & Relationships*, April 16, 2020.
https://www.mindbodygreen.com/articles/the-12-universal-laws-and-how-to-practice-them.

123 de Bruin, Marc. "Universal Laws; The Law of Polarity." *Simplifying Life*, Accessed on 2019.
https://simplifyinglife.com.au/the_law_of_polarity/.

124 Maxwell, John C. "Good Leaders Ask Great Questions, Your Foundation For Successful Leadership." *Center Street, Amazon*, October 7, 2014.
https://www.amazon.com/Good-Leaders-Ask-Great-Questions-ebook/dp/B00I829QJ8.

125 Jenquin, Marilyn. 1998. "International Foundation for Spiritual Knowledge (IFSK)." http://ifsk.org/.

126 Brown, Rosemary C. "Unfinished Symphonies." *Souvenir Press*, 1971. https://www.goodreads.com/book/show/1259198.Unfinished_Symphonies.
127 Wikipedia. "Ludwig van Beethoven." Accesssed on 2021. https://en.wikipedia.org/wiki/Ludwig_van_Beethoven.
128 Wikipedia. "Franz Liszt." Accessed on 2021 https://en.wikipedia.org/wiki/Franz_Liszt.
129 Wikipedia. "Frédéric Chopin." Accessed on 2021. https://en.wikipedia.org/wiki/Frédéric_Chopin.
130 Wikipedia. "Claude Debussy." Accessed on 2021. https://en.wikipedia.org/wiki/Claude_Debussy.
131 Wikipedia. "Robert Schumann." Accessed on 2021. https://en.wikipedia.org/wiki/Robert_Schumann.
132 Wikipedia. "Johann Sebastian Bach." Accessed on 2021. https://en.wikipedia.org/wiki/Johann_Sebastian_Bach.
133 Wikipedia. "Sergei Rachmaninoff." Accessed on 2021. https://en.wikipedia.org/wiki/Sergei_Rachmaninoff.
134 Wikipedia. "Johannes Brahms." Accessed on 2021. https://en.wikipedia.org/wiki/Johannes_Brahms.
135 Wikipedia. "Rosemary Brown (spiritualist)." Accessed on 2021. https://en.wikipedia.org/wiki/Rosemary_Brown_(spiritualist).
136 Arcilla, Imelda. 2011. "The RICH Playbook." https://www.ImeldaArcilla.com/.
137 Beckwith, Michael Bernard. 2019. "MichaelBeckwith.com." https://michaelbeckwith.com/.
138 Wikipedia. "Thomas Edison. " Accessed on 2019. https://en.wikipedia.org/wiki/Thomas_Edison.
139 Ferlazzo, Larry. "What Is The Accurate Edison Quote On Learning From Failure?" *LarryFerlazzo.com*, June 11, 2011. http://larryferlazzo.edublogs.org/2011/06/11/what-is-the-accurate-edison-quote-on-learning-from-failure/.
140 Clear, James. 2019. "JamesClear.com." https://jamesclear.com/.
141 Hoffower, Hillary. "The Same Question That Can Chart A Path To Early Retirement Is The One Warren Buffett Used

To Build Berkshire Hathaway Into A Powerhouse." *Business Insider*, March 14, 2019.
https://www.businessinsider.com/warren-buffett-business-strategy-set-path-to-early-retirement-2018-10.

142 Wikipedia. "Warren Buffett." Accessed 2019.
https://en.wikipedia.org/wiki/Warren_Buffett.

143 Wikipedia. "Charlie Munger." Accessed 2019.
https://en.wikipedia.org/wiki/Charlie_Munger.

144 Berkshire Hathaway. 2019. "BerkshireHathaway.com."
https://www.berkshirehathaway.com/.

145 Buffet, Warren. "2010 Annual Report." *Berkshire Hathway*, Published in 2011. Page 22-24.
http://www.berkshirehathaway.com/2010ar/2010ar.pdf.

146 Webster, Ian. "U.S. Inflation Rate, $1,000 from 1939 to 2020." *Official Data Foundation*, Accessed on 2020.
https://www.in2013dollars.com/us/inflation/1939?amount=1000.

147 Duncan, Christopher M. 2019. "The Conscious Education Company, The Magnetic Mind Method, and Author of You're Not Broken."
https://christophermduncan.com/.

148 Fritz, Robert. 1989. "Robert Fritz Inc."
https://www.robertfritz.com/wp/.

Chapter 8

149 Inspirational Stories. 2019. "Traditional Proverbs >>(About Art, Dreams, Society & Civilization)."
https://www.inspirationalstories.com/proverbs/traditional-a-civilization-is-as-great-as-its/.

150 Arcilla, Imelda. 2011. "The RICH Playbook."
https://www.ImeldaArcilla.com/.

151 Rassi, Brian. "enstigate™ funding solutions program." *enstigate.com*, Created in 2017.
https://www.enstigate.com/.

152 Wikipedia. "Pablo Picasso." Accessed on 2019.

https://en.wikipedia.org/wiki/Pablo_Picasso.
153 Psychology Iresearchnet.com. 2019. "Positive-Negative Asymmetry."
http://psychology.iresearchnet.com/social-psychology/social-cognition/positive-negative-asymmetry/.
154 Vaish, Amrisha; Grossmann, Tobias; and Woodward, Amanda. "Not all emotions are created equal: The negativity bias in social-emotional development." The *National Center for Biotechnology Information*; *Psychol Bull*, May 2008.
https://www.ncbi.nlm.nih.gov/pmc/articles/PMC3652533/.
155 Marano, Hara Estroff. "Marriage Math." *Psychology Today*, March 16, 2004.
https://www.psychologytoday.com/us/articles/200403/marriage-math.
156 Wikipedia. "Jim Rohn." Accessed on 2019.
https://en.wikipedia.org/wiki/Jim_Rohn.
157 Groth, Aimee. "You're The Average Of The Five People You Spend The Most Time With." *Business Insider*, July 24, 2012.
https://www.businessinsider.com/jim-rohn-youre-the-average-of-the-five-people-you-spend-the-most-time-with-2012-7.
158 Clemmer, Jim. "Innovation and the Law of Averages." *The Clemmer Group*, Accessed on 2019.
https://www.clemmergroup.com/articles/innovation-law-averages/.
159 Heart Math Institute. 2019. "HeartMath.com"
https://www.heartmath.com/.
160 Global Union Scientists For Peace. "Defusing World-Crises Selected References." *Gusp.org*, Accessed on 2019.
https://www.gusp.org/defusing-world-crises/selected-references/.
161 Rassi, Brian. "The ART Technique." *enstigate.com*, Created in 2017. https://www.enstigate.com/.
162 Wikipedia. "Mike Tyson." Accessed in 2019.
https://en.wikipedia.org/wiki/Mike_Tyson.

163 Hani, Julie. "The Neuroscience of Behavior Change." *Healthtransformer.co; Fit4D.com*, August 8, 2017. https://healthtransformer.co/the-neuroscience-of-behavior-change-bcb567fa83c1.

164 Proctor, Bob. 2019. "Bob Proctor." https://www.proctorgallagherinstitute.com/.

165 Huhem, Mitch. 2018. "MitchHuhem.com." http://mitchhuhem.com/bio/.

166 Ingerman, Sandra. 2019. "SandraIngerman.com." https://www.sandraingerman.com/.

167 Ingerman, Sandra. "Soul Retrieval: Mending the Fragmented Self." *Amazon*; *Harper One; Revised, Updated edition*, August 8, 2006. https://www.amazon.com/Soul-Retrieval-Mending-Fragmented-Self/dp/0061227862.

Chapter 9

168 Good Reads Inc. "Val Uchendu." Goodreads, March 23, 2017. https://www.goodreads.com/quotes/8201979-when-you-appl y-that-gift-you-possess-that-comes-so.

169 Wikipedia. "Global Positioning System (GPS)." Accessed on 2021. https://en.wikipedia.org/wiki/Global_Positioning_System.

170 Trank, Andrea. "Delete, Distort and Generalize: We all do it!" *Heavenlanecreations.com*, Jan. 17, 2021. https://heavenlanecreations.com/delete-distort-and-generalize-we-all-do-it/.

171 Duncan, Christopher M. 2019. "The Conscious Education Company, The Magnetic Mind Method, and Author of You're Not Broken." https://christophermduncan.com/.

172 Brainy Quote. "Denis Waitley." *BrainyQuote*, Accessed on 2019. https://www.brainyquote.com/quotes/denis_waitley_125740.

173 Meetup. 2019. "Meetup.com." https://www.meetup.com/.

174 Nelson, Dr. Bradley. "The Emotion Code." *Amazon*; *Wellness Unmasked Publishing First Edition*, June 15, 2017.

https://www.amazon.com/Emotion-Code-Bradley-Nelson/dp/0979553709.

175 Duncan, Christopher M. 2019. "The Conscious Education Company, The Magnetic Mind Method, and Author of You're Not Broken." https://christophermduncan.com/.

176 Rassi, Brian. "MeFormula: Personalized Solutions Made Easy." MeFormula.com, Published in 2011. https://www.meformula.com/.

177 Dean, Brian. 2017. "Caring Palms Massage and Reiki." https://www.caringpalms.com/.

178 Frezyield. "Kipendacho moyo ni dawa. What the heart desires is medicine to it." *Funnyardstick.wordpress.com*, August 11, 2013. https://funnyardstick.wordpress.com/2013/08/11/methali-za-kiswahili-swahili-proverbs-part-1/

179 April_Roberts299. "6 Impulse Factors." *Quizlet*, Accessed on 2019. https://quizlet.com/259878022/6-impulse-factors-flash-cards/.

180 Braden, Gregg. 2019. "GreggBraden.com." https://www.greggbraden.com/.

181 Wikipedia. "Wall Street." Accessed on 2019. https://en.wikipedia.org/wiki/Wall_Street.

182 Home Science Tools. 2019. "Water: States of Matter." https://learning-center.homesciencetools.com/article/states-of-matter/.

183 Perry, Justin. 2019. "You Are Creators." https://youarecreators.org/

184 GotQuestions.org. 2019. "What is the meaning of I AM WHO I AM in Exodus 3:14?" https://www.gotquestions.org/I-AM-WHO-I-AM-Exodus-3-14.html.

185 Wikipedia. "Masaru Emoto" Accessed on 2019. https://en.wikipedia.org/wiki/Masaru_Emoto

Chapter 10

186 Lipton, Bruce H. 2018. "BruceLipton.com." https://www.brucelipton.com/.

187 Evans, Suzanne. 2019. "Driven Inc." https://driveninc.com/about/.

188 Cascio, Christopher N.; O'Donnell, Matthew Brook; Tinney, Francis J.; Lieberman, Matthew D.; Taylor, Shelley E.; Strecher, Victor J.; Falk, Emily B. "Self-affirmation Activates Brain Systems Associated With Self-related Processing And Reward And Is Reinforced By Future Orientation." *Oxford Academic; Social Cognitive and Affective Neuroscience*, Volume 11, Issue 4, April 2016, Pages 621–629. https://academic.oup.com/scan/article/11/4/621/2375054.

189 Wikipedia. "Ryder Cup." Accessed on 2019. https://en.wikipedia.org/wiki/Ryder_Cup.

190 Kelley, Brent. "How Long Does It Take to Play a Round of Golf?" *Liveaboutdotcom*, March 26, 2018. https://www.liveabout.com/time-it-takes-to-play-a-round-1560498.

191 Orlando, FL. 2019. "Orlando.gov." https://www.orlando.gov/Home.

192 St. Petersburg, FL. 2019. "StPete.org." https://www.stpete.org/.

193 Craigslist. 2019. "Craigslist.org." https://www.craigslist.org/.

194 Jacksonville Beach, FL. 2019. "JacksonvilleBeach.org." http://www.jacksonvillebeach.org/.

195 Wikipedia. "Lou Holtz." Accessed on 2019. https://en.wikipedia.org/wiki/Lou_Holtz.

196 Wikipedia. "Notre Dame." Accessed on 2021. https://en.wikipedia.org/wiki/Notre_Dame_College.

197 Ismail, Rocket. 2021. "Rocket Ismail." https://rocketismail.com/index.html.

198 Bettis, Jerome. 2021. "Jerome Bettis." http://thebus36.com/.

199 Wikipedia. "Tim Brown." Accessed on 2021. https://en.wikipedia.org/wiki/Tim_Brown_(American_football).

200 Patrice Blanchot. "Lou Holtz Inspirational Speech." *Youtube.com*, Sept. 9, 2017. https://youtu.be/0wMmcoPTmAs.

201 Jones, Dennis Merritt. "Grow Deep and You'll Stand Tall." *HuffPost*, June 19, 2012. https://www.huffpost.com/entry/mindfulness-practice_b_1433344.

202 Jones, Dennis Merritt. "Strong Winds Strong Roots." *Natural Awakenings Publishing Corporation*, March 31, 2015. https://www.naturalawakeningsmag.com/Natural-Awakenings/April-2015/Strong-Winds-Strong-Roots/.

203 Dispenza, Joe. 2019. "DrJoeDispenza.com." https://drjoedispenza.com/.

204 Omega Institute for Holistic Studies. "Bruce H. Lipton: When You Understand a Cell, You Understand Humans." *Youtube.com*, April 18, 2007. https://youtu.be/9GaB1VMAXPQ.

205 Fortson, Leigh. "Epitgentics." *BruceLipton.com*, February 8, 2012. https://www.brucelipton.com/epigenetics/.

206 Lipton, PhD., Bruce H. "The Biology of Belief." *Amazon*, October 11, 2016. https://www.amazon.com/Biology-Belief-10th-Anniversary-Consciousness/dp/140195247X/.

207 Ariane. "What is Teachability Index And Why This Knowledge Can Change Your Life." *Steemit*, July 19, 2017. https://steemit.com/life/@ariane/what-is-teachability-index-and-why-this-knowledge-can-change-your-life.

Chapter 11

208 Arcilla, Imelda. 2018. "ImeldaArcilla.com." https://www.ImeldaArcilla.com/.

209 Wikipedia. "Human Intelligence." Accessed on 2019. https://en.wikipedia.org/wiki/Human_intelligence.

210 Wikipedia. "HU (mythology)." Accessed on 2019. https://en.wikipedia.org/wiki/Hu_(mythology).

211 Eckankar. 2019. "Experience HU: The Sound of Soul." https://www.eckankar.org/hu.html.

212 Harris, Catherine C. "The Egyptian God, Hu." *Tour Egypt*, Accessed on 2019. http://www.touregypt.net/featurestories/hu.htm

213 Arcilla, Imelda. 2018. "ImeldaArcilla.com." https://www.ImeldaArcilla.com/.

214 Enoch, Noctis. "Seven Levels of Intelligence and Three Types of Genius." *Mind Reality*, Accessed on 2019. http://www.mindreality.com/seven-levels-of-intelligence-and-three-types-of-genius.

215 Behrend, Genevieve. "Your Invisible Power." *Amazon; Rough Draft Printing*, January 4, 2013. https://www.amazon.com/Your-Invisible-Power-Genevieve-Behrend/dp/1603865136.

216 Troward, Thomas. "The Edinburgh Lectures on Mental Science." *Amazon; Martino Fine Books*; Illustrated edition, February 10, 2014. https://www.amazon.com/Edinburgh-Lectures-Mental-Science/dp/1614275688.

217 Boland, Jack. "12 Steps To A Spiritual Experience." Amazon; Master Mind Publishing Co., January 1, 1983. https://www.amazon.com/Twelve-Steps-Spiritual-Experience-Boland/dp/B000X8C3LI.

218 PSYCH-K Centre International. 2019. "Psych-k.com." https://psych-k.com/.

219 Duncan, Christopher M. 2019. "The Conscious Education Company and The Magnetic Mind Method." https://christophermduncan.com/.

220 Striecher, Colette. 2020. "ColetteStriecher.com." http://www.colettestreicher.com/about-colette/.

221 Ulanov, Ann Belford. "The Wizard's Gate: Picturing Consciousness." *Amazon; Daimon Verlag*; 1st edition, January 1, 1994.

https://www.amazon.com/Wizards-Gate-Picturing-Consciousness/dp/3856305394.
222 Rassi, Brian. 2018. "BrianRassi.com." https://www.brianrassi.com/.

Chapter 12

223 Wikipedia. "Robert Greene." Accessed on 2019. https://en.wikipedia.org/wiki/Robert_Greene_(American_author).
224 Wikipedia. "Phoenicia." Accessed on 2019. https://en.wikipedia.org/wiki/Phoenicia.
225 George, Rita. 2018. "RitaGeorge.com." http://ritageorge.com/.
226 Peoria Area World Affairs Council. 2020. "Pawac.org." https://www.pawac.org/.
227 Itoo Society, Inc. 2020. "Society.itoohall.com." http://society.itoohall.com/.
228 Peoria, IL. 2021. "Peoria, IL." http://www.peoriagov.org/.
229 Bradley University. 2020. "Bradley.edu." https://www.bradley.edu/.
230 Wikipedia. "Carl Jung." Accessed on 2019. https://en.wikipedia.org/wiki/Carl_Jung.
231 Holst, Sanford. April 30, 2011. "Phoenician Secrets: Exploring the Ancient Mediterranean." http://www.sanfordholst.com/phoenicians.htm.
232 Wikipedia. "United States." Accessed on 2019. https://en.wikipedia.org/wiki/United_States.
233 Rodriguez, Gregory. "How Genealogy Became Almost as Popular as Porn." *Time*, May 30, 2014. https://time.com/133811/how-genealogy-became-almost-as-popular-as-porn/.
234 Logical Levels Inventory. 2020. "Logical Levels Model." https://www.logicallevels.co.uk/pages/why-lli/logical-levels-model-1
235 Dilts, Robert. 2020. "NLP University International." http://www.nlpu.com/NLPU.html

236 Wikipedia. "Gregory Bateson." Accessed on 2019. https://en.wikipedia.org/wiki/Gregory_Bateson.
237 Fritz, Robert. 1989. "Robert Fritz Inc." https://www.robertfritz.com/wp/.
238 Wikipedia. "Coronavirus Disease (COVID-19)." Accessed on 2020. https://en.wikipedia.org/wiki/Coronavirus_disease_2019
239 RaintreeWriting.com. "Family Ecology Theory." Raintreewriting.com, Accessed on 2021. https://www.raintreewriting.com/a-3-paragraph-essay-example-about-family-ecology-theory.
240 Fan, Ryan. "Carrying The Emotional Burden of a Dysfunctional Family." *Medium.com*, July 22, 2019. https://medium.com/invisible-illness/carrying-the-emotional-burden-of-a-dysfunctional-family-b3e2e79a3b33
241 TraumaDissocaition.com. "Alters in Dissociative Identity Disorder." *Traumadissociation*.com, Retrieved Jun 19, 2021. http://traumadissociation.com/alters.
242 Lumen. "Introduction to Personality." *LumenLearning.com*, Accessed on 2021. https://courses.lumenlearning.com/boundless-psychology/chapter/introduction-to-personality/.
243 Tabac, Magda. "PCM Types of Personality." Magdabac.com, Accessed on 2021. https://magdatabac.com/process-communication-model-pcm/types-of-personality/.
244 YouTube. 2020. "YouTube.com." https://www.youtube.com/.
245 Trank, Andrea. "Delete, Distort and Generalize: We all do it!" *Heavenlanecreations.com*, Jan. 17, 2021. https://heavenlanecreations.com/delete-distort-and-generalize-we-all-do-it/.
246 Duncan, Christopher M. 2019. "The Conscious Education Company, The Magnetic Mind Method, and Author of You're Not Broken." https://christophermduncan.com/.

247 Sinek, Simon. 2019. "SimonSinek.com." http://simonsinek.com/.
248 Inside Quest. "The Millennial Question." *YouTube; Interview with Tom Bilyeu on Inside Quest*, Dec. 30, 2016. https://www.youtube.com/watch?v=vudaAYx2IcE.
249 Impact Theory. "Tom Bilyeu." Accessed on 2021. https://impacttheory.com/.
250 Dean, Brian. 2017. "Caring Palms Massage and Reiki." https://www.caringpalms.com/.
251 Arcilla, Imelda. 2018. "ImeldaArcilla.com." https://www.ImeldaArcilla.com/.
252 Morrissey, Mary. 2019. "Life Mastery Institute." https://www.lifemasteryinstitute.com/.
253 Enstigate.com. 2020. "Success Guide Masterclass." http://www.enstigate.com/success-guide-masterclass/
254 Insight State's Editorial. "3 Levels of Consciousness – Three Levels of Mind – Conscious, Subconscious and Superconscious." *Insightstate.com*, March 14, 2021. https://www.insightstate.com/spirituality/3-levels-consciousness-three-levels-mind/.

Dictionary

255 Wikipedia. "Google Dictionary." Accessed on 2019. https://en.wikipedia.org/wiki/Google_Dictionary

Acknowledgements

256 Arcilla, Imelda. 2018. "ImeldaArcilla.com." https://www.ImeldaArcilla.com/.
257 Oberbrunner, Kary. 2019. "KaryOberbrunner.com." https://karyoberbrunner.com/.
258 Author Academy Elite. 2019. "Author Academy Elite." https://authoracademyelite.com/
259 Reiss, Laura. 2021. "CruxOrganizing.com." https://www.cruxorganizing.com/.

260 Jenquin, Marilyn. 1998. "International Foundation for Spiritual Knowledge (IFSK)." http://ifsk.org/.
261 Phillips, Crystal. 2020. "Ladybug on a Leaf Designs." https://www.etsy.com/uk/shop/ladybugonaleaf.
262 George, Rita. 2018. "RitaGeorge.com." http://ritageorge.com/.
263 Hazlehurst, Taylor. 2019. "Taylor Hazlehurst." https://www.linkedin.com/in/taylorhazlehurst/
264 Matlin, Carey. 2019. "TenFourMediaGroup.com." https://tenfourmediagroup.com/.
265 The Guild. 2019. "Authors Academy Elite The Guild." https://authoracademyelite.com/the-guild.
266 Duncan, Christopher M. 2019. "The Conscious Education Company, The Magnetic Mind Method, and Author of You're Not Broken." https://christophermduncan.com/.
267 Covey, Stephen. 2019. "Stephen Covey." https://stephencovey.com/.

About the Author Brian Rassi

268 Rassi, Brian. 2018. "BrianRassi.com." https://www.brianrassi.com/.
269 Enstigate.com. 2017. "Enstigate.com." https://www.enstigate.com/.

About Imelda Arcilla

270 Arcilla, Imelda. 2018. "ImeldaArcilla.com." https://www.ImeldaArcilla.com/.

Your Next Steps with Mastering Success

271 Enstigate.com. 2020. "Success Guide Masterclass." http://www.enstigate.com/success-guide-masterclass/
272 Enstigate.com. 2021. "Accelerator Guide Program." https://www.enstigate.com/accelerator-guide-program
273 Enstigate.com. 2020. "Capital Guide Program." https://www.enstigate.com/capital-guide-program

274 Enstigate.com. 2020. "Growth Guide Program." https://www.enstigate.com/growth-guide-program
275 Matlin, Carey. 2019. "TenFourMediaGroup.com." https://tenfourmediagroup.com/.
276 Rassi, Brian. "MeFormula: Personalized Solutions Made Easy." MeFormula.com, Published in 2011. https://www.meformula.com/.
277 Rassi, Brian. 2018. "BrianRassi.com." https://www.brianrassi.com/.

DICTIONARY [255]

A

Action (/ˈakSH(ə)n/noun)

1. the fact or process of doing something, typically to achieve an aim.

Affirmation (/ˌafərˈmāSH(ə)n/noun)

1. the action or process of affirming something or being affirmed.
2. emotional support or encouragement.

Alchemy (/ˈalkəmē/noun)

1. the medieval forerunner of chemistry, based on the supposed transformation of matter. It was concerned particularly with attempts to convert base metals into gold or to find a universal elixir.
   a. Similar: chemistry, magic, sorcery, witchcraft, enchantment.
2. a seemingly magical process of transformation, creation, or combination.

Align (/əˈlīn/verb)

1. place or arrange (things) in a straight line.
2. give support to (a person, organization, or cause).

Appearance (/əˈpirəns/noun)

1. the way that someone or something looks.
2. an act of performing or participating in a public event.

Art (ärt/noun)

1. the expression or application of human creative skill and imagination, typically in a visual form such as painting or sculpture, producing works to be appreciated primarily for their beauty or emotional power.
2. a skill at doing a specified thing, typically one acquired through practice.

ART (Brian Rassi's acronym)

1. Align Raise Transform

Assign (/əˈsīn/verb)

1. allocate (a job or duty).
2. designate or set (something) aside for a specific purpose.

Attraction (/əˈtrakSH(ə)n/noun)

1. the action or power of evoking interest, pleasure, or liking for someone or something.
2. a quality or feature that evokes interest, liking, or desire.
3. a place which draws visitors by providing something of interest or pleasure.
4. a force under the influence of which objects tend to move toward each other.

Awareness (/əˈwernəs/noun)

1. knowledge or perception of a situation or fact.
2. concern about and well-informed interest in a particular situation or development.

B

Being (/ˈbēiNG/noun)

1. existence.
2. the nature or essence of a person.
3. a real or imaginary living creature or entity, especially an intelligent one.

Belief (/bəˈlēf/noun)

1. an acceptance that a statement is true or that something exists.
2. trust, faith, or confidence in someone or something.

C

Certainty (/ˈsərtntē/noun)

1. firm conviction that something is the case.
2. the quality of being reliably true.
3. a fact that is definitely true or an event that is definitely going to take place.

Competence (/ˈkämpədəns/noun)

1. the ability to do something successfully or efficiently.

Conscious (/ˈkän(t)SHəs/adjective)

1. aware of and responding to one's surroundings; awake.

2. having knowledge of something; aware.
3. painfully aware of; sensitive to.

Contrast (/ˈkänˌtrast/noun)

1. the state of being strikingly different from something else in juxtaposition or close association.

Creation (/krēˈāSH(ə)n/noun)

1. the action or process of bringing something into existence.

D

Desire (/dəˈzī(ə)r/noun)

1. a strong feeling of wanting to have something or wishing for something to happen.
2. strongly wish for or want (something).

Devotion (/dəˈvōSH(ə)n/noun)

1. love, loyalty, or enthusiasm for a person, activity, or cause.
2. religious worship or observance.
3. prayers or religious observances.

Direction (/dəˈrekSH(ə)n/ noun)

1. a course along which someone or something moves.
2. the management or guidance of someone or something.

Doubt (/dout/noun)

1. a feeling of uncertainty or lack of conviction.

E

Ego (/ˈēgō/noun)

1. a person's sense of self-esteem or self-importance.
2. Psychoanalysis: the part of the mind that mediates between the conscious and the unconscious and is responsible for reality testing and a sense of personal identity.
3. Philosophy: (in metaphysics) a conscious thinking subject.

Enlightenment (/inˈlītnmənt/noun)

1. the action of enlightening or the state of being enlightened.

Entity (/ˈen(t)ədē/noun)

1. a thing with distinct and independent existence.

Emotion (/əˈmōSH(ə)n/noun)

1. a natural instinctive state of mind deriving from one's circumstances, mood, or relationships with others.
2. instinctive or intuitive feeling as distinguished from reasoning or knowledge.

Entrepreneurship (/ˌäntrəprəˈnərˌSHip/noun)

1. the activity of setting up a business or businesses, taking on financial risks in the hope of profit.

Evolve (/ēˈvälv/verb)

1. develop gradually, especially from a simple to a more complex form.

2. (with reference to an organism or biological feature) develop over successive generations as a result of natural selection.

Existence (/igˈzistəns/noun)

1. the fact or state of living or having objective reality.

Expansion (/ikˈspanSHən/noun)

1. the action of becoming larger or more extensive.

Experience (/ˌikˈspirēəns/noun)

1. practical contact with and observation of facts or events.
2. the knowledge or skill acquired by experience over a period of time, especially that gained in a particular profession by someone at work.
3. an event or occurrence that leaves an impression on someone.

F

Failure (fālyər/noun)

1. lack of success.
    a. Synonyms: lack of success, nonfulfillment, defeat, collapse, foundering, etc.
2. the omission of expected or required action.

Faith (/fāTH/noun)

1. complete trust or confidence in someone or something.
2. strong belief in God or in the doctrines of a religion, based on spiritual apprehension rather than proof.

Fear (/ˈfir/noun)

1. an unpleasant emotion caused by the belief that someone or something is dangerous, likely to cause pain, or a threat.

FEAR (acronym)

1. Failed Expectations that Appear Real

Feeling (/ˈfēliNG/noun)

1. an emotional state or reaction.
2. a belief, especially a vague or irrational one.

Free will (noun)

1. The ability or discretion to choose; free choice.
2. The power of making choices that are neither determined by natural causality nor predestined by fate or divine will.

Fulfillment (fü(l)-ˈfil-mənt/noun)

1. the act or process of fulfilling
2. the act or process of delivering a product (such as a publication) to a customer.

G

God (/gäd/noun)

1. (in Christianity and other monotheistic religions) the creator and ruler of the universe and source of all moral authority; the supreme being.
2. (in certain other religions) a superhuman being or spirit worshiped as having power over nature or human fortunes; a deity.

Greedy ('grēdē/adjective)

1. having or showing an intense and selfish desire for something.
2. having an excessive desire.

Guidance (/'gīdəns/noun)

1. advice or information aimed at resolving a problem or difficulty, especially as given by someone in authority.
2. the directing of the motion or position of something, especially a missile.

H

Happy (/'hapē/adjective)

1. feeling or showing pleasure or contentment.
   a. having a sense of confidence in or satisfaction with (a person, arrangement, or situation).
   b. satisfied with the quality or standard of.
   c. willing to do something.
   d. (of an event or situation) characterized by happiness.
   e. used in greetings.
2. fortunate and convenient.

Happiness (/'hapēnəs/noun)

1. the state of being happy.

Higher Self

1. Higher self is a term associated with multiple belief systems, but its basic premise describes an eternal, omnipotent, conscious, and intelligent being, who is one's real self.

2. Blavatsky formally defined the higher self as "Atma the inseparable ray of the Universe and oneself. It is the God above, more than within, us." Each and every individual has a Higher self.[1]

HU (/He/Sufism)

1. Hu or Huwa ("He") is a name for God in Sufism. ... In Sufism Hu or Huwa is the pronoun used with Allah or God and is used as a name of God. Allah Hu means "God, Just He!" In Arabic Allah means God and with Hu, as an intensive added to Allah, means "God himself."
2. In Egyptian ancient culture HU meant God-Creator so we are Godman.

I

Incompetence (/inˈkämpədəns/noun)

1. inability to do something successfully; ineptitude.

Infinite (/ˈinfənət/adjective)

1. limitless or endless in space, extent, or size; impossible to measure or calculate.

Influence (/ˈinflo͝oəns/noun)

1. the capacity to have an effect on the character, development, or behavior of someone or something, or the effect itself.

Inner (/ˈinər/adjective)

1. situated inside or further in; internal.
2. mental or spiritual.

Intelligence (/inˈteləjəns/noun)

1. the ability to acquire and apply knowledge and skills.
2. the collection of information of military or political value.

Intuition (in·tu·i·tion/noun)

1. the power or faculty of attaining to direct knowledge or cognition without evident rational thought and inference.
2. quick and ready insight

Inversion (/inˈvərZHən/noun)

1. the action of inverting something or the state of being inverted.
2. a reversal of the normal decrease of air temperature with altitude, or of water temperature with depth.

J

Judgement (/ˈjəjmənt/noun)

1. the ability to make considered decisions or come to sensible conclusions.
    a. an opinion or conclusion.
    b. a decision of a court or judge.
2. a misfortune or calamity viewed as a divine punishment.

K

Knowing (/ noh-ing/adjective)

1. affecting, implying, or deliberately revealing shrewd knowledge of secret or private information.

2. that knows; having knowledge or information; intelligent.
3. shrewd, sharp, or astute.
4. conscious; intentional; deliberate.

L

Lack (/lak/noun)

1. the state of being without or not having enough of something.

Lack Direction – (definition from the Cambridge Dictionary)

1. to not know what you really want to do

M

Magic (/ˈmajik/noun)

1. the power of apparently influencing the course of events by using mysterious or supernatural forces.
2. mysterious tricks, such as making things disappear and appear again, performed as entertainment.
3. a quality that makes something seem removed from everyday life, especially in a way that gives delight.

MAGIC (Imelda Arcilla's acronym)

1. Multi-dimensional Alignment with God's Infinite Creation

Master (/ˈmastər/adjective & verb)

1. having or showing very great skill or proficiency.
2. main; principal.

3. acquire complete knowledge or skill in (an accomplishment, technique, or art).
4. gain control of; overcome.

Meditate (/ˈmedəˌtāt/verb)

1. think deeply or focus one's mind for a period of time, in silence or with the aid of chanting, for religious or spiritual purposes or as a method of relaxation.

Meditation (/ˌmedəˈtāSH(ə)n/noun)

1. the action or practice of meditating.
2. a written or spoken discourse expressing considered thoughts on a subject.

Mind (/mīnd/noun)

1. the element of a person that enables them to be aware of the world and their experiences, to think, and to feel; the faculty of consciousness and thought.
2. a person's intellect.

Multidimensional (/ˌməltēdəˈmen(t)SH(ə)n(ə)l /adjective)

1. of or involving several dimensions or aspects.

N

Natural Law (noun)

1. a body of unchanging moral principles regarded as a basis for all human conduct.
2. an observable law relating to natural phenomena.
3. is a philosophy asserting that certain rights are inherent by virtue of human nature, endowed by

nature—traditionally by God or a transcendent source—and that these can be understood universally through human reason. As determined by nature, the law of nature is implied to be objective and universal; it exists independently of human understanding, and of the positive law of a given state, political order, legislature or society at large.

O

Observation (/ˌäbzərˈvāSH(ə)n/noun)

1. the action or process of observing something or someone carefully or in order to gain information. a remark, statement, or comment based on something one has seen, heard, or noticed.

Outer (/ˈoudər/adjective)

1. outside; external.

P

Path (/paTH/noun)

1. a way or track laid down for walking or made by continual treading.

Polarity (/pōˈlerədē/noun)

1. the property of having poles or being polar.
2. the relative orientation of poles; the direction of a magnetic or electric field.
3. the state of having two opposite or contradictory tendencies, opinions, or aspects.

Problem (/ˈpräbləm/noun)

1. a matter or situation regarded as unwelcome or harmful and needing to be dealt with and overcome.
2. an inquiry starting from given conditions to investigate or demonstrate a fact, result, or law.

Purpose (pər-pəs/noun)

1. something set up as an object or end to be attained : INTENTION
2. a subject under discussion or an action in course of execution

Q

Quality (qual·i·ty/noun)

1. peculiar and essential character
2. degree of excellence
3. social status

Quantity (quan·ti·ty/noun)

1. an indefinite amount or number.
2. the aspect in which a thing is measurable in terms of greater, less, or equal or of increasing or decreasing magnitude.
3. duration and intensity of speech sounds as distinct from their individual quality or phonemic character.

R

Raise (/rāz/verb)

1. lift or move to a higher position or level.
2. increase the amount, level, or strength of.

Resistance (/rə'zistəns/noun)

1. the refusal to accept or comply with something; the attempt to prevent something by action or argument.
2. the ability not to be affected by something, especially adversely.

RICH (Imelda Arcilla's acronym)

1. Reclaim your Integrity to Create Happiness

S

Self (/self/noun)

1. a person's essential being that distinguishes them from others, especially considered as the object of introspection or reflexive action.

Skill (/skil/noun)

1. the ability to do something well; expertise.
2. a particular ability.

Solution (/sə'lo͞oSH(ə)n/noun)

1. a means of solving a problem or dealing with a difficult situation.
2. the correct answer to a puzzle.
3. products or services designed to meet a particular need.

Soul (/sōl/noun)

1. the spiritual or immaterial part of a human being or animal, regarded as immortal.
2. emotional or intellectual energy or intensity, especially as revealed in a work of art or an artistic performance.

Source (/sôrs/noun)

1. a place, person, or thing from which something comes or can be obtained.
    a. a spring or fountainhead from which a river or stream issues.
    b. a person who provides information.
    c. a book or document used to provide evidence in research.
    d. a body or process by which energy or a particular component enters a system.
    e. a part of a field-effect transistor from which carriers flow into the inter-electrode channel.

Spirit (spir-ət/noun)

1. an animating or vital principle held to give life to physical organisms.
2. a supernatural being or essence: such as HOLY SPIRIT, SOUL sense
3. temper or disposition of mind or outlook especially when vigorous or animated in high spirits.
4. the immaterial intelligent or sentient part of a person.

State - (/stāt/noun)

1. the particular condition that someone or something is in at a specific time.
    a. a physical condition as regards internal or molecular form or structure.

State of Being (/noun)

1. The overall physical condition of a person, as opposed to mental condition (state of mind).

Subconscious (/səbˈkänSHəs/adjective)

1. of or concerning the part of the mind of which one is not fully aware, but which influences one's actions and feelings.

Success (/səkˈses/noun)

1. the accomplishment of an aim or purpose.
2. the attainment of popularity or profit.
3. a person or thing that achieves desired aims or attains prosperity.

Superconscious (/ˌso͞opərˈkänSHəs/adjective)

1. transcending human or normal consciousness.

T

Thought (/THôt/noun)

1. an idea or opinion produced by thinking, or occurring suddenly in the mind.
2. the action or process of thinking.

Transform (/tran(t)sˈfôrm/verb)

1. make a thorough or dramatic change in the form, appearance, or character of.

Trust (/trəst/noun)

1. firm belief in the reliability, truth, ability, or strength of someone or something.

Truth (/tro͞oTH/noun)

1. the quality or state of being true.
2. that which is true or in accordance with fact or reality.
3. a fact or belief that is accepted as true.

U

Uncertainty (/ˌənˈsərtn(t)ē/noun)

1. the state of being uncertain.

Unconscious (/ˌənˈkänSHəs/adjective)

1. not conscious.

Universe (/ˈyo͞onəˌvərs/noun)

1. all existing matter and space considered as a whole; the cosmos. The universe is believed to be at least 10 billion light years in diameter and contains a vast number of galaxies; it has been expanding since its creation in the Big Bang about 13 billion years ago.
    a. a particular sphere of activity, interest, or experience.

Unlack (/un-lack/adjective)

1. to remove lack

V

Vibration (/vīˈbrāSH(ə)n/noun)

1. an instance of vibrating.
2. physics: an oscillation of the parts of a fluid or an elastic solid whose equilibrium has been disturbed, or of an electromagnetic wave.
3. informal: a person's emotional state, the atmosphere of a place, or the associations of an object, as communicated to and felt by others.

Visualization (/ viZH(o͞o)ələˈzāSH(ə)n/noun)

1. the representation of an object, situation, or set of information as a chart or other image.
2. the formation of a mental image of something.

W

Worry (/ˈwərē/verb)

1. give way to anxiety or unease; allow one's mind to dwell on difficulty or troubles.

Y

You (yü/pronoun)

1. the one or ones being addressed.
2. ONE sense

Yo-yo (yō-(ˌ)yō/noun)

1. a thick grooved double disk with a string attached to its center axle that is made to fall and rise to the hand by unwinding and rewinding on the string
2. a condition or situation marked by regular fluctuations from one extreme to another
3. a stupid or foolish person

INDEX

B

C

D

E

R

T

U

V

W

Y

ACKNOWLEDGMENTS

"To be you is an act of sacred rebellion."
—Imelda Arcilla [256]

There are truly several souls who I want to fully express my greatest gratitude to. The first is to my best friend, greatest partner in life, and truly the wisest person I have ever been around, Imelda Arcilla. Your love is still felt beyond all realms, dimensions, timelines, and lifetimes!

Her magic is to instigate life through her sacred being. In this very act, she created a sacred rebellion that will have a ripple effect beyond comprehension. It affected me, and now it has affected you. With great gratitude and appreciation, the universe, Imelda, and I want to thank you for accepting the life-changing devotion to MAGIC. Unlack yourself so you can unlock more success in your life.

The second soul I want to acknowledge is my own, for continuing to do whatever it took to get my attention to remember the truth. I want you to know, soul, that I have received your message loud and clear! It's time to put into action the very purpose of why I am here in the first place. Buckle up, self, because it's going to be a good ride, to say the least!

Third, I want to thank my connection to God, Source, and the universe itself. How could I complete such a compilation of information without your direct guidance? I want to say thank you for co-creating it with me. Also, I want to thank all my guides, ancestors, and friends who continued to act accordingly to connect the dots and cross the T's as well.

Next, I want to thank my publisher and author coach, Kary Oberbrunner of Author Academy Elite, for his incredible insight and intent to help ignite as many souls as possible! I knew immediately when you first spoke that you were the right person in which to join forces. Thank you for putting together a team (aka Erica Foster) and a mission of such high caliber that the only logical conclusion is to produce in that manner. [257-258]

I want to thank all my beta readers Laura Reiss, Marilyn Jenquin, Carey Matlin, Crystal Phillips, Rita George, Taylor Hazlehurst, Danielle Arcilla, Virginia Rassi, and Jen George for their incredible insights and suggestions to better shape the flow of the content. [259-263]

Carey Matlin, Ten Four Media Group, for her amazing book cover design, images, website, back ads and photos. [264] Nannette O'Neal and Nansi Krauss, from The Guild, for both their amazing editing skills and insight to help bring the book together. Virginia Rassi for her relentless editing eyes along the many reiterations of the book's journey to this point. [265]

Christopher M. Duncan, founder of The Magnetic Mind Method and author of You're Not Broken, for his wonderful foreword and incredible insights along the way. Special thanks to The Conscious Education Company team for their training and support in my Magnetic Mind Certification.[266]

I want to acknowledge and thank all my family, friends and associates over the years. Our direct interaction has had a compound effect that was the burning desire to share my deepest thoughts in the first place. How could I dedicate decades of experiences and not share the knowledge obtained to help my fellow being? As per Stephen Covey, "To know and not to do is not to know." [267]

Finally, special thanks to Imelda's parents Lily and Michael Jay. Robert and Danielle Arcilla and their sons Alex and Noah. My parents Tim and Virginia Rassi, the Trinacty Family (Angi Rassi, Brent, Grace, John, and Hannah Trinacty), Craig and Mandy Rassi and their children Kaitlyn, Nick, and Giuliana, and our cats Nina and Kali for their love and support over the years. Imelda and I truly appreciated it!

ABOUT THE AUTHOR

Brian Rassi's purpose is to be a catalyst–an agent for accelerated success in both life and business. An author, coach, trainer, speaker, and entrepreneur, he earned a reputation as "manifesting generator" when it comes to the entrepreneurial world and growing leaders in the business community.

Brian has navigated, uncovered, and successfully implemented ancient wisdom that is relevant to anyone who is seeking improvement, both personally and professionally. He is the CEO and Co-founder of enstigate™ with decades of experience that has taken him into many industries and unique circumstances. [268-269]

Not the traditional route for sure. In fact, it's been a humbling journey for him to experience the wisdom gained from various business projects, industries, and the wearing of different hats.

What he has gained is the fortunate edge in being able to handle challenges, from numerous angles, to move a project forward, and many times, to success where others would give up.

Whether in sales, management, teamwork, leadership, operations, marketing, or mindset, he found solutions that are normally un-tapped. He helps others break through limits in what's possible for a prosperous outcome, no matter the circumstance.

When he is not running enstigate™ or traveling to speak, Brian can usually be found at home mastering his craft in whatever area he feels will enhance his life to the fullest.

Connect at brianrassi.com or enstigate.com

ABOUT IMELDA ARCILLA

Within each one of us is a seed of stardust, and when properly nourished, we become luminous beyond words, helping to set the world on fire in the most beautiful and inspiring way.

In the early 2000s I had an out of body mystical experience you hear about that changes the landscape of your life forever. I truly understood that the universe is inside each one of us. And everything we're searching for is within, waiting to be activated through desires and experiences.

Ever since then, I have been unpacking the universe, which is love, wisdom, and intelligence—with some divine magic of course!

I have a holistic approach and don't fit in a conventional way. I see life in a deeper interconnected way beyond the surface. Like the universe, I am many things and so are you.

I am a mystic, creative entrepreneur, angel, and star-soul. Like many, I have sensed a life beyond planet Earth. With all this, I am grounded, humbled to assist others with my wisdom to discover your greatest destiny and potential.

I am here to nourish your spirit and activate your soul with light to live more brilliantly and boldly your dreams. Basically, my MAGIC elevates your MAGIC!

I ascended in June 2017. I am now a Transcended Soul and Spirit able to help you at any moment. If you came to this page, most likely it is time for you to evolve and remember why you are here! [270]

For more information go to ImeldaArcilla.com

List of Imelda Arcilla's Quotes for Quick Reference:

"MAGIC doesn't happen on the well-traveled path!"

"Turn your focus from being scared
to a sacred being that you truly are!"

"Multi-dimensional Alignment with
God's Infinite Creation"

"Reclaim your Integrity to Create Happiness"

"Devotion is the superpower that sustains the rigorous challenge. It is the light in your corner that fuels your endurance to go the distance."

"Your soul evolves through entrepreneurship"

"You're just on the other side of what you want."

"To be you is an act of sacred rebellion."

YOUR NEXT STEPS WITH MASTERING SUCCESS [271-277]

SUCCESS GUIDE

NEED HELP LEARNING THE ART AND SCIENCE OF MASTERING SUCCESS?

Holding onto success in life is NOT easy sometimes. If you tried before and failed, don't worry, it's not your fault society and the self-help industry misled you. That's why we created the *SUCCESS GUIDE*, the mindset masterclass program designed to *HELP YOU EASILY CREATE A LIFE THAT YOU LOVE:*

- Weekly Masterclass schedule designed to CONNECT to your own intuition.
- Easy-to-follow, FLEXIBLE, daily planning system based on transforming vision into result.
- End MINDSET and SUCCESS STRUCTURE confusion.
- Easy, fast, SUPERCONSCIOUS RECODE sessions that release limiting beliefs in minutes.
- 24/7/365 access to an ONLINE INSTITUTE with 88+ hrs. of on-demand videos.
- ACCOUNTABILTY and support is provided to ensure successful manifestations.
- GUARANTEED results to create more flow in your life and business.

The SUCCESS GUIDE is available to those individuals and businesses who want to experience growth immediately without wasting time!

AVAILABLE AT
ENSTIGATE.COM/SUCCESS-GUIDE-MASTERCLASS

ACCELERATOR GUIDE

CREATE IMMEDIATE MOMENTUM IN THE RIGHT DIRECTION

It's possible to go from zero to mach 10 in a very short amount of time. In fact, when placed in the right structures you can almost feel the momentum begin to create a compound effect within you! That's why we decided to create the ACCELERATOR GUIDE, the life and business program designed to GET YOU IN POSITIVE MOTION WITHIN DAYS-TO-WEEKS NOT MONTHS-TO-YEARS:

> IMMEDIATE ALIGNMENT With Both Your Personal and Business True Choices.

> Build a Money Access Plan (MAP) with Complete CLARITY ON HOW You Will Obtain It.

> Be Able to Define and Implement the Right Amount of HEALTHY STRUCTURES Into Your Daily Experience.

> Tap into Our Powerful CAPITAL DATABASE NETWORK with Endless Ways to Accelerate Your Business Now.

> Quickly TRANSFORM BY CREATING New Habits and Holding Yourself Accountable for Your Own Success.

> Easy, Fast, SUPERCONSCIOUS RECODE Sessions That Release Limiting Beliefs in Minutes.

> EXPERIENCE What It Feels Like When You Have A Team Initiating Your Vision into A Reality.

The ACCELERATOR GUIDE is available to those business owners and entrepreneurs who want QUICK RESULTS WITH THE MOST IMPACT.

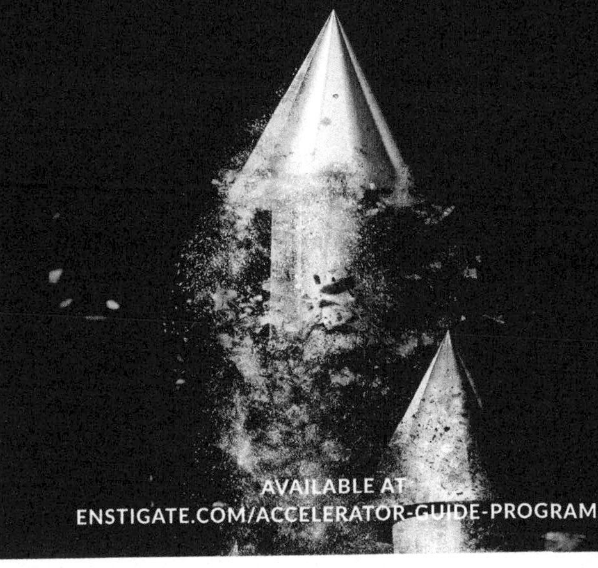

CAPITAL GUIDE

ACCESS THE RIGHT MONEY. AT THE RIGHT TIME. IN THE RIGHT WAY!

No matter if you're starting or trying to expand a business it takes access to capital to do it properly. A lot of times entrepreneurs and business owners end up spinning their wheels chasing the money. They go about it all wrong; they just don't know what to do and they lose momentum of the dream that inspired them to take action in the first place. That's why we created the CAPITAL GUIDE, the complete capital accessing program designed to HELP YOUR BUSINESS ACCELERATE NOW!

> Proven funding solution with CUSTOMIZED Business Plan, Proforma, and Pitch Deck!
> In-house UNDERWRITING and write-up to ensure you get approved quickly!
> Endless DATABASE of Capital Sources Looking to Place Money Now.
> Accelerate Your Business Rapidly with this CAPITAL access program.
> Dedicated Team Member to help GUIDE you through the capital process.
> 24/7/365 access to an ONLINE MEMBERSHIP with an 8+ Hrs. of On-Demand Videos.
> Weekly Business Coaching, Success Mindset and ACCOUNTABILTY Support.

GROWTH GUIDE

TAKE YOUR BUSINESS TO THE NEXT LEVEL!

You're either growing or dying. At some point in the business you realize it's time to bring on more help. That decision brings with it multiple unforeseen growing pains that can easily be eliminated with the right structures in place. That's why we created the GROWTH GUIDE, the composite business solution program designed to HELP YOU FINALLY FULFILL YOUR VISION AND MISSION FOR THE BUSINESS!

> Business GROWTH Consulting with Live One-on-One Video Calls every Month.
> Strategic Business STRUCTURING and Equity-Growth Strategy.
> PROPRIETARY Cash-Flow, Liquidity-Enhancing and Debt-Elimination Structure.
> Cost Remediation Service, SAVINGS Analysis and Professional Support.
> ACCESS the Right Money, at the Right Time, in the Right Way!
> Business Credit Builder System with STEP-BY-STEP direction.
> Weekly Business Coaching, Success Mindset and ACCOUNTABILITY Support.

The GROWTH GUIDE is available to those entrepreneurs and businesses who lack the available resources to get the solutions they need to scale so they can experience ongoing success.

TEN FOUR
DEDICATED TO GROWING BUSINESSES

TENFOURMEDIAGROUP.COM

PERSONALIZE YOUR LIFE

AROUND YOUR OWN NEEDS AND WANTS

AVAILABLE AT
MEFORMULA.COM

BRIAN RASSI

AUTHOR, SPEAKER, AND MANIFESTING GENERATOR OF GROWTH AND SUCCESS

Brian helps individuals and companies to be successful, to be better leaders, and grow their vision through the fine art of life-changing mastery. Each presentation is a successful-learning experience with powerful research, engaging storytelling, and actionable strategies for measurable results. Brian has navigated, uncovered, and successfully implemented ancient wisdom that is relevant to anyone who is seeking improvement, both personally and professionally. Areas of Interests for speaking workshops, training and coaching:

- Learn the Art and the Science of Mastering Success.
- Discover What, Why, and How Lack Affects Your Behaviors.
- How Best to Navigate Entrepreneurship and Business Ownership.
- What Really Motivates a Team and How to Improve Your Leadership Abilities.
- How to Implement Accountability into an Organization and Why It Improves Productivity.
- Why You Must Systemize Your Processes and How to Do That Effectively.
- How to Access the Right Money, At the Right Time, In the Right Way for Your Business.

"Known Brian for a few years, he is truly special and amazing! He comes from many different levels as it relates to business understanding. Mind, body, spirit and he brings all of that into the business realm... Brilliant!"

- Carolyn Greenleaf, All Things Wellness Expo

"Brian has very extensive knowledge about how funding works for every level of Entrepreneur and Business Owner. He delivered another great speech about funding and many of our Members and Partners have built relationships with him and he has helped many of them with their funding needs in 2019."

- Tom Jikomes, Power Networking Club Expo

Made in the USA
Middletown, DE
27 November 2021